Love After 40

How to fall in love in the age of Tinder.
A book for women
who don't believe in love.

Iwona Kulwicka

An author of her own life,
entrepreneur who introduces order
in business and private life,
the happiest of mothers,
wonderful woman
falling in love with herself and life.

Iwona Kulwicka

Love After 40

How to fall in love in the age of Tinder.
A book for women
who don’t believe in love.

2024

Translation: Monika Rola
Proofreading: Monika Rola
Technical Correction: Karolina Kadluczka
Cover and graphic design: Joanna Lamek
Cover photo: Julita Ledzinska
Text Compostion: InkWander

ISBN: 9788397063044

Limitless Mind Publishing Ltd
15 Carleton Road
Chichester
PO19 3NX
England
Tel. +44 7747761146
Email: office@limitlessmindpublishing.com

Dear Reader!

Find us on Facebook/Instagram:
limitless mind publishing

And visit our page on Amazon
by entering: limitless mind publishing into the search bar
or by scanning the QR code to see our other titles.

♥*We would greatly appreciate your opinion. It means a lot to us.*

TABLE OF CONTENT

* * *

March.

7:15 a.m. - I just found out it's over. I was stricken by these words, fixed to the kitchen chair for several minutes.

So what did I do?

Did I get mad, call him a bastard, plan sweet revenge?

No! Nothing of the sort.

Instead, I considered ending my life…

Thankfully, the universe must have been watching over me because, in a moment of my darkest thoughts, I was saved by a phone call from a friend.

Why would I give up on life?

A long, toxic relationship in which we danced like two addicts led me to the moment when I came to believe that without that man:

I AM NO ONE - I HAVE NOTHING-
I DON'T MATTER - I AM A ZERO…

* * *

One look.
A slight tightness in the throat, a short twinge of the heart,
Cupid's arrow!
Will I follow it?
Will I sail out into the ocean of not-always-easy experiences,
Or will I stay on the safe shore?
Will I give myself a chance to feel what is untamed and deepest,
Will I be content to wade in the pool of everyday life?
What will I choose?
No, I won't be afraid anymore!
I set course for deep waters.

Introduction - Excuse me, could I object?

A few months later.

I'm packing! It's quite a task to fit everything into a carry-on bag. Ha, ha.

"What's everything?" – you ask.

Good question. What is "everything" when your trip is supposed to last just a weekend? The answer, of course, depends on where and towards whom you are traveling. Hi, hi.

I pack my black velvet high heels and favorite cream dress with puffed sleeves, jeans, a jacket, and sneakers.

"Where are you going?" You ask.

I'm sure that once I add a satin nighty to my bag, together with lace underwear and stockings, the purpose of my trip will become pretty obvious.

Tonight, I jump into my bed exceptionally quickly. Why? To get some sleep before traveling? No, more to calm my anxiety, to fall asleep and not think about tomorrow.

I don't feel well. My joints hurt, and I'm sure I have a low-grade fever. This is too much. I've been waiting for this trip for so long. Will I have to give it up? I load up on vitamin C and drink hot water with garlic, ginger, and lemon. I accept no option other than that I will be on a plane to Bologna, Italy, tomorrow at 12:20 pm.

Nothing can stop me!

* * *

What won't we do for love?

I can do a lot. I'm still learning what I won't do, learning my limits. I like being in love because it awakens creativity and sensitivity and makes me curious about what other emotions I might experience next.

It's midnight, and my eyes, open wide as two full moons, stare at Warsaw's beautifully lit Palace of Culture and Science. I can see it from my bedroom window. I toss and turn, daydreaming about what could happen tomorrow. Fifteen minutes go by, then 15 more, and so on.

"I have to stop this, no more overthinking" - I tell myself. I turn on relaxing music, and after a while, like a beautiful white cloud, my long-awaited sleep arrives.

* * *

As I go about my morning routine, I'm visited by an old friend. Fear. Once upon a time, we were roommates, fear and me, but he only occasionally crashes at my place these days. It's fascinating how intuitively he chooses the moments for his visits. Fear knows me intimately and knows when I am most vulnerable to his suggestions. He luxuriates in my head then, as if relaxing in a comfortable recliner. He crosses his legs. He clasps his hands and asks with a sneer:

"What's the point of this trip?"

"Are you sure he will pick you up at the airport?"

"What do you expect from a guy you've only known for such a short time?"

"Aren't you afraid?!"

Yes! I am afraid!

"What are you afraid of?"

Disappointment. Two months of waiting to meet my sweetheart gave me much time to build up expectations and profound feelings. What will

I do if my perfect Fulvio turns out to be just a figment of my imagination? How will I react if it turns out that I idealized him?

I decide not to engage in a depressing conversation with Fear. To banish it, I call up my courage. The courage that I got from my family. From my father, who never gave up, and my grandmothers, who were epitomes of strength.

My trust in life, which is slowly returning to me, allows me to gain distance and recognize my fear for what it is - an irrational echo of pain from the past.

* * *

I'm at the airport very early. I buy water and a sandwich. I sit down on one of the available chairs and start writing. Shortly after, two women sit behind me. I can't see them yet, but I hear their conversation.

They're friends going on vacation to Florence. One is clearly very unhappy. She has just left her boyfriend after a relationship that lasted three years. She can't shake off the pain of it.

I hear her ask herself: "How could he do this to me?"

The breakup is all the more painful because her boyfriend left her for another woman - a school friend. Grief and resentment pour out with every word she speaks.

"Do you know what he told me?" - she vents. "I did so much for him! I tailored my entire life to suit him! I even arranged time with my children so that it fell when he had other things to do. If I made any plans, I would tell him about them far in advance so he couldn't accuse me of not caring about him or abandoning him to loneliness. He didn't respect me and was constantly jealous of everything. And I tried so hard! I loved him so much, and I still love him. I don't see the point of life without him! He was my constant companion. I had someone to go on vacation and go to the movies with. I was not alone. And now? Who will want me now?! I was so happy with him. I miss him so much!"

Her friend tries to comfort her and promises support.

"You and I will go on vacations together" - she promises. "You'll see, you'll forget about this once you get busy with something. We just need to find a way to keep you occupied."

The friend dishes about her own relationship. She's with a man she doesn't love, although she really likes him. She encourages her unhappy friend to forget about romantic goals by saying:

"I often talk to my boyfriend about love and falling in love. I'm as big a romantic as you and dream of loving and feeling loved. I still feel that longing for something exciting, for butterflies in my stomach and that wonderful vibe accompanying them. Still, I've started to wonder if my boyfriend is right… He believes that we should forget about falling or being in love after age fifty. People should be happy with a relationship that's mostly friendship at this age. Falling in love and being in love is for young people, not for us. He keeps telling me that the sooner I come to terms with it, the less I'll be disappointed in the long run. He believes love should be replaced by respect and trust at a certain age.

He's asked me:

- What's the point of the other stuff?
- What's the point of foolish elation and euphoria?
- Who actually needs it?
- You just end up feeling pain!
- Isn't it better to just live in peace and stability?"

At that moment, I remembered the words of Jacek Walkiewicz, author of the book *The Full Power of Possibilities:* "Sztaudynger once wrote: *A pin brings stability to the butterfly.* This is why if someone - regardless of how old they are - sets such a goal (to bring stability to themselves or a business), they're on a road to nowhere. This is a trap. Please remember that. We grow and we conquer experiences only when we go beyond our comfort zone... A person can only experience something new only by entering somewhere new..."[1]

The boyfriend's philosophy on love saddens me. It reminds me of twenty years ago when, on my thirty-fourth birthday, I announced to my party guests that I never wanted to fall in love again. I remember exactly how I felt at that moment. I was angry, broken, and unhappy.

I asked myself, "What's so nice about being in love?"

And I replied: "It's just suffering. I prefer to live in peace, without unnecessary excitement and stress."

To this day, I hear the echo of my cold and pointed words, fuelled by fear of emotions that are not always easy.

In the airport seats behind me, the conversation continues:

"Stop stressing, please. Honestly, set aside daydreams about falling in love and look for someone with whom you can settle and relax into old age."

I couldn't help myself. I turned slightly, looked over my shoulder, and said:

"Excuse me, ladies, could I object? Forgive me for butting in; I wasn't trying to eavesdrop, but I couldn't help hearing your conversation and felt I had to say something. I don't mean to intrude. I just wanted to say that falling in love after fifty is beautiful and possible. It's not easy, but it is beautiful. I will turn fifty-four years old in two days, and I am actually on my way to meet my Italian lover in Bologna."

When I finished, the women's faces lit up. I could see a sparkle in their eyes, their cheeks flushed, and wonderful, joyful smiles appeared. They looked as if they had found the meaning of existence and looked as if they had received thc news that tickets for another type of life were now on sale.

Of course, we had to fall into a deep conversation. Who could resist moving towards it when you see the light at the end of the dark tunnel?

---

[1] Translated from original Polish. Jacek Walkiewicz, *Full Power of Possibilities*, Helion, Gliwice 2015, s. 10.

We became immediate friends, the easy, conspiratorial energy being shared between the three of us making the rest of the passengers assume we had known each other for a long time and were traveling together.

"Where did you meet your Italian friend?" – Magdalena (or Magda for short), as I learned was the name of the upset friend, asked.

"On Tinder."

"Oh no." - she replied. "I've checked it out too, but either I don't like them, or I'm afraid they won't like me. Besides, how can I know if someone is the guy for me when all I have are pictures of him?"

"True. You won't know until you meet. The secret, however, is that if you don't feel a spark on the first date, you don't have to go on the second one. You can change your mind whenever it feels right, even after four dates. People sometimes leave relationships after thirty years together, and that's not bad either. Of course, that's a hard thing to go through, but everyone is free to do it. Matters of the heart are our own individual domain, and other people should respect our choices. Please remember only your opinion matters here. Give yourself the chance to have that first date."

Magda lightly ran her hand over her forehead, brushed aside her closely cropped bangs, and smiled in disbelief.

"And it works?"

"Definitely. You're looking at an example of it working. I met Fulvio just after I broke up with another Italian guy. His arrival in my life has been a great surprise and a wonderful gift. I didn't suspect that I would fall in love. He showed up and stayed. See how amazing it is. You meet a man on Tinder, go on just two dates with him, and return to your home country, and even though everything seems to indicate that the distance will end the short romance, two months pass, and we are still together."

"That's amazing" – said Magda.

"Opening yourself up to dating again will give you some distance from your last relationship and show you that there are many nice people in this world. I bet that you'll feel more confident when you notice that you have attributes others find attractive. Getting out there again is a great motivator - to take care of yourself, to learn something new, to fill that void that a breakup can leave"- I advised. "Just don't put pressure on yourself and your new partners. My advice is to resist the urge to immediately assess if he would be good husband material. Go with the flow of the adventure. Maybe you will find something there. Maybe you will discover a common passion for photography or cooking. Who knows? You might gain a great friend even if you have no spark. There are plenty of fish in the sea; you can always fish again."

"How nice to meet someone with such a fresh perspective in such an unusual way!' - the other friend, Beatrice, said. "You're giving us hope that life can be beautiful and full of adventure after 40, 50, and beyond. What a gift to meet such a positive and sincere person. Thank you!"

Magda added:

"Today, I had a real revelation. You've convinced me there is still a chance for something I had long lost hope for. For love."

Our conversation lasted over two hours. After arriving in Bologna, we hugged each other warmly and went our separate ways.

The lesson I learned: **Speak up. You never know when you could give someone else courage and inspiration.**

The lesson you learned is:

....

....

....

....

....

....

....

....

....

....

....

....

....

....

....

....

....

....

....

....

....

....

....

....

....

....

....

....

La Dolce Vita

We met on Tinder.

Him – a Sicilian with an angelic face and divine eyes, whose photos immediately caught my attention.

What was it that arrested me?

Beautiful, sincere, and deep eyes, a wonderful carefree smile full of child-like joy.

Fulvio – lover of motorcycle travel and photography.

I – a Polish woman with hair blonde as sunshine, a new admirer of Italy, looking for a soft place to land after my last breakup.

It's weird; I wonder why I've fallen in love with Italy so intensely only now. I've been a tourist here many times. I've visited Rome and Naples and watched breathtaking concerts at the Opera di Verona. I've basked in the sun on the beaches of Sirmione and Rimini and indulged my vanity with shopping in Milan. However, something about Italy recently grabbed my heart and imagination. I can't stop thinking about this place.

My friend Aldona has asked me many times already:

"Why can't you just find a guy at home?"

Because my dear. Because something is drawing me here subconsciously. Because it's just happening, and why not? Because even though I did not plan any of this, life brought me here.

* * *

When I first saw Florence in May this year, it felt like homecoming. I found fascination everywhere. In the atmosphere of Italian street life. In the Italian spontaneity and joy for life. In the simple but divine food that I enthusiastically ate here with my hands, in the ancient architecture filled with echoes of the past. All of it felt like home to me.

Standing before the Basilica Santa Croce, I scanned each of her frescoes, each carefully carved sculpture. I felt as if I was checking that nothing had changed there, that everything was as it was before, in its place. Admiring a panorama of the city, I cried like a soldier returning to his family home after a long sojourn. I couldn't explain what I felt.

Just like I can't explain why, out of the hundred men whose profiles I had viewed and liked, I went on a date with Fulvio.

You could call it an accident or a coincidence. I, however, don't believe in coincidences anymore. I believe that all our experiences have a purpose.

When I saw his profile, I liked it immediately. He didn't look like a sex bomb, nor did he boast about his Ferrari; instead, he held a camera in his hand. He had something that captivated me - a beautiful and sincere smile.

What now? – I thought.

Total silence, slight uncertainty, and clandestine curiosity.

Will he like me, too?

I waited seconds, but it felt like forever.

Yes! He tagged me, too! He likes me! Wonderful!

“Bingo!” - I shouted joyfully, unaware that this story would have twists and turns.

* * *

Dating app users rarely discuss the emotional charge they feel while surfing websites. However, there are some people out there who describe it as a kind of addiction.

They say: “I'm taking some time off Tinder because I’m getting too into it” or “I’m taking a break because I spend too much time on here.”

“Why would dating apps be addictive?” – you ask.

Well. You have moments where you feel like the master of life and death. The choice of candidates is in your hands. You, and only you, decide whose profile you will like and who you will reject. Perhaps you find satisfaction in feeling a form of power and control, sometimes comparable to that which your parents and teachers had over you? Or maybe classifying men into those who are and are not worthy of your attention - after seeing only a few photos - feels like revenge for all of your heartbreaks from the past?

“I just don't like him” you explain a rejection. “I have the right to choose. I don't have to like everyone.”

Then again, although you may be stunningly beautiful and confident, the moment you like an online dating profile, you immediately start to wonder how they’ll judge you. When a match happens, you’re happy, maybe even elated. These first few moments “after” are full of adrenaline and endorphins, which you can get hooked on and need more each day just to feel like you’re worth something. Often, the feeling of being chosen is all a person needs. You might not even care about the potential date and may not be searching for love. Instead, you use the situation to tend to your wounded inner child.

* * *

The first time he contacted me, just like so many others, he sent me a smiley face and asked me what I was doing in Italy.

"I'm on vacation."

"How long will you be here?"

"I leave Bologna on Saturday…"

"On no, Saturday? So soon?"

"Yep, but today is only Wednesday."

"True! We have a few days to meet.

Full of excitement, we immediately confirmed the date and location for our first date.

On Thursday, at 8:03 am, I'm awoken by the following text message:

"Good morning, Sweetheart. Are you ready to meet?"

"Si."

"Wow. I feel like a teenager."

"Me too."

"Oooooh, yeah!'"

**All conversations with Fulvio were in English*

He sent me some photos from his last vacation to make sure I knew who I was about to meet. I sent him mine for the same purpose. You can't always trust profile photos from dating sites. I've heard more than one story about someone excited to meet someone tall, dark, and handsome, only to find the exact opposite waiting for them.

* * *

I felt like a teenager anticipating that first date.

What should I wear? What should I do with my hair?

I'd been on a few dates before, but none had made me so excited and nervous. I spent all morning anticipating the good fortune that fate would hopefully bring me and feeling anxious that it may turn out to be just a small and meaningless distraction.

OK. I'm ready. I've settled on high heels and my white dress with a blue houndstooth pattern. When I ordered it in an online store a year ago, I had no idea it would become a date outfit. Just like I couldn't predict, photos from my last vacation in Florence and on the island of Elba would be the perfect addition to my online dating profile. I remember one day, I spontaneously took a great selfie. I didn't know why I was doing it, but I felt I needed to capture this moment and this place.

"You look phenomenal" - I heard from my sister, with whom I spent the last week of my vacation in Modena, Italy. "I'm keeping my fingers crossed for you. Good luck and have fun, dear."

Then, at Cindirella's ball, the clock struck midnight. Except my midnight was 4 p.m., the time of our date. The hour struck, and I was struck by fear. Each tick of the clock brought questions that attacked my intelligence, denied my feminine allure, and questioned the wisdom of being open to new experiences.

"What's the point of going?" Fear whispered.

"He's younger than you." Fear noted pointedly.

"Maybe he's just a kid?" He tried to turn me off the whole idea.

"This is nonsense..."

Fear didn't get to finish the last sentence because I interrupted his depressing monologue with a decisive:

"Enough! Stop this! I've made my decision, and I'm going!" I shouted.

A notification arrived on WhatsApp with a message from my Italian:

"I'm here!"

He's here!

I was staying on the second floor. *Should I take the elevator or run down the stairs?* - I asked myself and then zoomed down the stairs like a teenager. I was being carried by an energy of excitement and joy. I felt alive. I ran to the gate, smiling from ear to ear. The world was spinning around me. My senses sharpened. I heard the birds singing in the oleander bush covered with pink flowers; I felt the wind gently caress my shoulders, and from a distance, the smell of a blooming acacia tree called to me. My eyes opened wide and sparkled in the rays of the Italian sun.

I wasn't sure exactly where he would be waiting for me. I approached the nearest parked car, tilted my head slightly, looked into the side window and... Oh, my! I was greeted by a smile as sweet as a Sicilian orange and chocolate eyes looking at me. An elegantly shaped beard touched with white frost, a neatly trimmed mustache, a shaved head. The face of a child and a man in one. Such a lovely combination.

His "Hey, sweety!" almost knocked me off my feet. I felt an express train pass over my head and then an intoxicating silence. The feel of his voice moved every part of me. As if the pianist, striking the keys assuredly, sent vibrations through my body as I hung suspended in the music notations. Never before had a man's voice made such an impression on me.

I got into the car, knelt on the passenger seat, leaned over Fulvio, and gently pulled his chin toward me, giving him a sweet kiss. I tasted him.

I used to have no idea that you could feel the taste of a man, that after the first time you buried your lips in his, you could find the certainty that this was something. Something so hard to describe in words. Some call it a state of *flow*, others call it an energy, and I call it destiny. A mutual agreement to experience something new and unknown.

I placed my lips gently on his lips, slightly parted in invitation. They were soft and juicy like fresh peaches from a Florence market. I covered them with my lips, gently pressing and releasing as if I wanted to extract at least a little nourishing sweetness from them.

He touched my hair shyly. Combed it with his tanned hands and stroked it as if he wanted to draw the last rays of summer from them. Gently ran his fingers across my face, brushing away a stray curl that got in the way of him looking into my eyes. I felt like I was in heaven. There was a romantic silence around. I could hear his steady and clear breathing. His heart beat faster and faster. I placed my hands on his shaved head, drawing irregular patterns with my fingers to leave my mark on him. All my perception moved to my fingertips. I tuned them to such sensitivity that I'd discover every irregularity of his skin.

Would I decide to do something bolder? Maybe I'd touch his neck? Perhaps I'd put my hands on his hairy chest? Maybe I'd let him know immediately that I felt close to him.

Our lips were only the first stop of our rapture. My azure eyes, filled with the Italian sun, sparkled, waiting for his next look. I looked at him. Looked so deeply that finally, I saw nothing. I only felt - warmth, the beating of my heart, and butterflies in my stomach.

* * *

We head out on our date.

By the time we're eating Gelato, we eat not like friends but like lovers. We share our flavours with each other. We play, taking alternating licks of his vanilla and my chocolate. I get a feeling. This is no ordinary meet-up.

A walk through the ancient streets of Modena makes me feel nostalgic and deeply moved. There is beauty all around me, a dear man beside me, and within me - peace.

We sit at a table in an Italian restaurant.

I love the bustle of Italian streets, where every alley emanates the love and joy of life. Feasting together, enjoying each other's company, appreciating the here and now. I am fascinated by how passionately Italians talk about cooking and eating. Like any topic, even the most trivial one, it can spark a passionate discussion. I don't speak Italian, but I can catch on to the meaning of conversations. Italians use more than just words to communicate. They talk to each other with their eyes, gestures, and whole body.

Beautiful weather and atmospheric music. Waiters bustle around and pay compliments to the guests. Here, each visitor feels cared for. We ordered a traditional Italian aperitif and some snacks. We sit next to each other. Fulvio caresses my hands, examining them as if he wants to remember every detail as if he is painting a precise picture of them in his mind. He touches each of my fingers in turn, each joint, each fingertip. I never knew it could feel so pleasant.

I feel present in the moment.

Every brush of my hair, every seemingly random movement of his hand on my back, sends shivers through me. I daydream about him touching my hips and thighs. My body demands caresses. I shyly run my fingers over his well-proportioned, more boyish than masculine hand. I gently grab the raven hair, covering it with my fingertips. It's like chocolate frosting on an Italian latte.

I place my hand in his as if to check if… Yes! Fits perfectly!

How much time can I dedicate to the celebration of a touch? I'd answer - "All of eternity!"

I feel his skin as if it were mine. Like something known, loved, belonging to me. Like something I've found after many years of searching. I lean my head over his shoulder. I take a deep breath and inhale his scent.

A slightly almond scent with a hint of lime and a bit of sweetness is picked up by my nose and moves further into me. It reaches my soul. I close my eyes to burn this scent into my memory. Our lips meet again. We flow in a common touch. The evening passes too quickly.

Second date? Yes! Urgently and necessarily, as I like to say. Urgently - because I don't want to live without this rapture any longer, and necessarily - because this feeling has become necessary for me like water to flowers, like flowers to butterflies, like butterflies to people sensitive to beauty.

We don't know yet that we have just set out on the most remarkable journey, called infatuation.

I've never smoked or tried drugs, and I only drink alcohol occasionally. Still, I think infatuation hooks you even faster than they do. What you feel in the moment of infatuation, what it triggers in your body and brain - is the highest level of bliss that can be achieved.

The day ends with a message from him on WhatsApp:

"Hey, Sweetie. Meeting you was fantastic."

I'm on cloud nine.

* * *

On Friday, he wakes me up at 8:03 am again:

"Hello, my sweet. Are you ready to spend another day with me?"

"Si."

"Me too."

I rise, my heart buoyant and my smile gleaming with anticipation. Today, I will see him again, feast my eyes on his presence, be enveloped in his intoxicating scent, and let his voice be my guide. Eagerly, I await the moment when I can surrender fully to the overwhelming tide of emotions within me.

I eat my breakfast lazily. Lost in recollections of yesterday's experiences, I carefully chew each bite of my oatmeal.

"Is this real? Is such a thing even possible?" - I ask.

Yes, it's possible and real because I feel it. Denying what I've found here and now would be like denying that you're alive. What you see, hear, and feel is the real world.

There is a growing sentiment that dwelling on past memories or future aspirations isn't the crux of life. Instead, it's vital that we feel alive, that we immerse ourselves in every moment, and engage all our senses. The power of living in the present lies in releasing our hold on what was or might be in favor of reveling in the joy of the here and now. This focus on the present, the only realm that's tangible and accessible to us, the only realm over which we have real influence.

My therapist Julia keeps telling me:

"Listen to your body, pay attention to how it reacts, observe it. The body never lies. It can tell us a lot. We just need to be mindful and open to feeling."

Ready for another lesson in mindfulness and feeling, I wait for my meeting with Fulvio. It's in five minutes.

Will I choose the elevator this time? Or the stairs again? I could run down like a joyful girl, awaiting something extraordinary, or like a frivolous fifty-year-old, hoping for excitement? I choose the stairs. Yes, that's the right choice. I celebrate the moment when each step I climb down brings me closer to Fulvio. I smile to myself. It's funny and revealing how little you need to be happy.

I peak nervously.

"*Is he there?*" I ask myself.

Yes. Fulvio is waiting for me by his car. He gallantly opens the door for me, invites me inside, and gently brushing my hair, he asks:

"Are you OK, my sweet? Ready to go?"

His demeanor and his voice melt me like warm chocolate fondue. On the one hand, he seems gentlemanly, noble, and elegant. On the other, he has a boyish gentleness and vulnerability. He doesn't know it yet, but I already have a feeling that I will set sail on my cruise through an ocean of profound experiences in a moment.

"What would you say to an invitation to my favorite restaurant?" he asks. "It's quaint and comfy."

I nod my head in agreement.

We spend the car journey mostly in silence, sometimes interrupted by breathing and other times by conversations about life. I am surprised by my reaction to the feel of his voice and the depth of his gaze and small gestures.

Suddenly, we're breaking hard, and his hand flies to protect me from hitting my head against the window. His reflexes and attentiveness amaze me. If it weren't for him, our date could have ended in the hospital.

"I'm so sorry, I'm so sorry for breaking so hard. I had no choice" he explains.

Once we get to the restaurant, we feed each other Italian delicacies. Aromatic finocchiona salami from Tuscany with a deep, delicious flavour. Seasoned with garlic, salt, pepper and stuffed with aromatic fennel, it pairs perfectly with Florentine salt-free bread. I wrap pieces of Parmigiano-Reggiano - a cheese with a divine, sweet, and sour taste - in slightly salty prosciutto from the same region and bring them to the mouth of my Italian beau. In return, he slides a spoon filled with snow-white and mildly creamy burrata between my lips. We have fun feeding each other cherry tomatoes and red peppers warmed in the southern Italian sun.

Dear moment, please last forever!

When I later tell my sister Aleksandra about what happened on the second date, she looks at me and says:

"Oooh, I don't recognize you, sis! Were you feeding each other on your second date? Just four months ago, you had trouble even sending a man a kissy-face emoji, and now… Well, well."

"Yep, I did it, my love. I did what I felt and wanted, and I'm proud that my rules and superstitions didn't stop me. I would have regretted it if I had chickened out. That's for sure."

"Tell me everything" said Aleksandra, sitting on the sofa. Her hazel-green eyes filled with curiosity.

"What I felt. Aaaaaaah." I sighed. "You'd never believe it…! I can't describe it." I added.

* * *

I had no doubts about my desire for him, my yearning to experience the warmth of his skin against mine. I was curious about my reaction when his hairy torso would hug my bare breasts and belly. Had he not made the first move, I would have initiated our intimate encounter.

It started with fervent kisses on the sofa, our lips engaging more intensely than ever before. His tender, warm tongue gently explored my neck and cleavage. Surrounded by the lazily flowing music from the Italian SkyRadio and the wonderful smell of Italian fragrances that spread throughout the apartment, we started our love dance.

I sat astride him, wrapped my thighs around his hips, and looked deep into his eyes. He froze.

"Is something wrong?" he asked.

"Not at all" I responded softly. "I just wanted to really see you" I added, maintaining eye contact. In his eyes, I could see a mix of bewilderment and awe.

He spoke up again:

"What's going on?"

"I can't take my eyes off you" I whispered.

In this moment, I let emotions take the reigns. I gently stroked his head, touched his cool earlobes, kissed his eyes, which were now closed with excitement, and his flushed cheeks. I dug my fingers into his lush but soft beard, slowly pulling his lips towards mine.

I paused to look deeply into his eyes again. I looked at him carefully as if I was framing a photo for a family album. I wanted to keep this image in my memory forever.

He gently took off my blouse and kissed my breasts, ready to receive his caresses.

I like this. This view when a man leans over me, slowly kisses my shoulders and neckline, until, in full excitement, he sinks his hot mouth into my also feverish body.

I didn't even notice when we were standing in front of each other, only in our underwear. Now, he took the initiative. He grabbed my hand and led me…

The bedroom welcomed us with a carefully made bed and the lovely scent of almonds, lime, and a bit of sweetness.

No more waiting. We hurriedly took off the remains of our clothes. I heard a delighted "Wow!" when he saw me only in lace undies. "Your body is beautiful" he said.

He then embraced me and gently laid me down. He touched me passionately. Stroked my feet, ankles, and calves. Moved his sensitive hands over my belly, neckline and neck.

Then he returned his attention to my thighs and whispered:

"You are like a ripe peach. Your skin is wonderful, soft, and delicate. I could touch you forever."

He slipped a determined hand under my panties and hurriedly took them off. He leaned his head over my belly, placed a few sweet kisses on it, and slowly and carefully kissed lower and lower.

He placed his mouth on my womb for a moment so that I could feel delight. I'd been waiting for this touch, this brush, after which a wave of desire welled in me. A rising rush of ecstasy that could no longer be stopped. I heard him say softly:

"You're so sweet. I adore the taste of you."

Now, warm hands reached for my lips. A delicious shiver ran through my body. I squirmed as if in ecstasy, trying to hold on to this state of adoration for him and for myself as long as possible. After a while, his fingers penetrated my insides. The Italian master of ceremonies needed just a few seconds to find the spot. I wanted more and more. "Dear moment, please last forever" I whispered. Anticipating my orgasm, I pressed his hand tightly against my womb. He wrapped his arms around me tightly and hugged me to him, and in this tangle of bodies, I experienced pleasure. He looked at me carefully, smiled, and asked:

"Would you like more?"

"Yes, I'm a long-distance runner" I replied.

He smiled again, looked deeply into my eyes, raised his body over me, and slowly sank into me with reverence and gentleness.

"Ah" he sighed.

I held him tightly against me, and my hands melted into his furry back.

"Ah" he sighed again, and I gently pinched his cool bum and whispered quietly, "Go, go, go."

"Don't close your eyes. Look at me" I asked. I no longer saw a shy boy but a man whose pleasure gave him virility and imbued him with masculine energy. I was in seventh heaven.

"*I feel so good with him and close to him*" I thought.

As he laid on his back and I, sitting on him, gave myself over to pleasure, he said:

"I wish I had a picture of you leaning over me and looking at me like this. I'll have to make one with my mind and keep it forever."

After our intoxicating closeness, we lay down next to each other. Not long ago, we had been nearly strangers. Now, we were lovers in an embrace, hands intertwined in unity. A true miracle of the energy of love…

* * *

I stopped recounting the story here and glanced conspiratorially at my sister.

"So, it was wonderful" - she summed it up.

"Yes, it was wonderful, but the most beautiful moment was yet to come" I added mysteriously.

"Oooh, what could that be?" - she asked with burning curiosity.

"Dearest…" - I began with a flourish as if I was about to review the second act of a world-famous play.

* * *

While Fulvio lay on his back and rested in a light half-sleep, I did nothing but look at him. I just... Hmm. I don't know what it is, and I don't know why, but... I couldn't take my eyes off him. I felt like I was in a trance, as if I was hypnotised and nourished by his sight, energy, and breath. First, I gently brushed my fingers against his clearly defined jet-black eyebrows. I traced the arch of his nose so that, by way of his flushed cheeks, I could gently fall onto his full lips that tasted of Sicilian oranges. I placed my hands in such a way that, without losing contact, I could hug and stroke his beard at the same time. His lush yet soft stubble tickled my fingertips. I could have stayed like this forever.

I snuggled into his chest, entwined his thighs with mine, and, giving into total trust in the here and now, I breathed steadily. Each exhale freed me more from overthinking, and each inhale filled me with bliss.

There was silence around me. My mind was still, my heart felt warm, and my soul recited my favorite prayer: "Dear moment, please last forever."

* * *

When I finished the story, there was a telling silence in the small apartment in Modena. I saw great emotion in my sister's eyes.

"That's beautiful" she said.

The lesson I learned is: It doesn't matter when and how you find love.

The lesson you learned is:

Polish Balance

My life waited for me in Poland. Family, friends and work.

I'm sure things will never be the same as before I met Fulvio. I'm trying to manage my hyperactivity caused by falling in love. I deal with my swirling thoughts by throwing myself into work. Heartsickness is best soothed by memories of beautiful moments spent together. The only thing I can't find an antidote to is my heated longing. Unfortunately, my fiery Italian isn't a prolific writer or conversationalist.

I receive a "We'll meet soon" - from him without a word about when or where, which baffles me. He contacts me daily, but only with "Good morning" and "How are you feeling?"

Occasionally, he sends warm messages: "I miss you" "I desire you" and "I still feel your taste" – but it's not enough for me. I want more and more.

I wait impatiently for a chat with my therapist and friend, Julia, hoping it will bring me relief. We meet on Zoom, and I hear her curiosity:

"Tell me, darling, what's happened?"

When I nod meaningfully, she is sure this is no ordinary vacation. Seeing and feeling my vibe, she has no doubt that a lot had happened. I tell her everything, adding at the end:

"I'm dreaming about seeing him again, about feasting on the sight of him, the feel of him, on the melody of his voice. Listen…" I stop and play a WhatsApp message he recorded.

Julia listens very carefully.

"Beautiful, warm and very authentic" - she describes the feel of Fulvio's voice.

"Yes. He has a manner in his voice that intrigues me" - I go back to explaining. "When he talks to me… Phew!… I'm sorry, but I need to take a breath. I can not. Look at me... I wonder why this man found me?! Why did the universe send him to me?! I've got myself into quite the turmoil" I say with trepidation and excitement. "He didn't write to me yesterday, and I cried so much. I cried, feeling bad for myself. I cried that I wouldn't see him again and wouldn't be able to feel what I experienced in Bologna" - I tell her, tears showing up again.

* * *

When Fulvio hadn't sent me a single message throughout the very long Saturday and an endless Sunday, I surrendered to anxiety. I felt frozen and couldn't function. Eventually, I broke and sent him a voice message:

> Fulvio. You don't write, you don't answer my messages. If you've changed your mind and don't want to keep in touch with me, please be upfront with me and don't keep me in suspense. It's difficult for me to live with not knowing.

I didn't have to wait for a response long. My sweet Sicilian wrote:

> "Hello dearest. Nothing has changed, and nothing has happened. I went to a motorcycle rally with my friends and came back very late and very tired. I haven't changed my mind about you or us at all. Don't fret. I had some issues at the office today, but everything is fine now. Call me, write, send messages whenever you'd like. Sending tight hugs and kisses."

* * *

Julia listens.

"I've noticed that I could listen to his voice messages round the clock. When he asks to talk to me, I melt… How can I regain some balance in all of this? I'm freaking out! Help me!"

My therapist's answer surprises and shocks me.

"Darling, read his text messages to your heart's content and stop judging yourself for it. Do what nourishes you. Falling in love can sweep any of us off our feet. That's normal and OK, you don't have to fear it. Sometimes, reading messages from your sweetheart is like having a dialogue with him. If your man's words nourish you, read them. Celebrating words is okay. Revel in what nourishes and elevates you. The speed of life has caused us to lose the ability to do this. To our great detriment, we do not give ourselves time to celebrate words these days. In the past, when there was no television or other entertainment when a woman in a village wrote a poem or a letter, all its inhabitants met to read it together. They read it daily, and the beauty they experienced during these meetings strengthened them."

I listen to her calmly and with amazement at the depth of these words. I sit silently and raise my head skeptically as she continues:

"Please, give yourself permission to experience falling in love. Women who come out of experiences like yours, after long-term relationship trauma, often internalize feeling that they're unworthy. If you say those words to yourself, tell yourself repeatedly that you don't deserve to be happy, that energy will drag you down, and you'll stop yourself from having a chance at a different life.

Tell yourself repeatedly: I've traveled a long road and deserve to be loved. I deserve for people to speak kindly to me and surround me with love. I deserve to feel bathed in love and live in happiness, health, and affection.

Believe that you deserve these things. In your life, you've shown care and respect to your parents and everyone else you know. That's what makes you deserving to accept goodness."

"I'm so drawn to Fulvio…" I say with nostalgia in my voice.

"That's beautiful!" Julia exclaims.

"...but I'm afraid" I add.

"Why?" Julia asks.

"Because I'm afraid I'll fall in love with him, and he'll... hmmm... If he wrote more often and kept in closer contact with me, I would have fallen in love a long time ago" I explain.

Julia looks at me. She closes her eyes, takes a deep breath, and says:

"OK, let's consider. Would it be good if you were in love right now with a very committed and fully present man who is at your every beck and call? Think about it: would you be able to appreciate it in the emotional state you are in now? Would this energy be alive and real?"

I closed my eyes for a moment, took a deep breath, and then I understood. She's right.

"If you look closely at it" she continued, "you'll see that if Fulvio was closer to you, you would immediately start judging him and looking for flaws in him. You still have a lot of different hang-ups that would immediately make themselves known.

You came to him as an independent woman, and don't change that. Stand firm in it. Don't go back to old behaviour patterns!"

"Old behaviour patterns?" I ask.

"Don't diminish yourself for him. You will lose everything. I know it's hard to remain strong, but you must do it. This man is challenging you to stand in complete, feminine independence, not in the energy of a child."

"True. I've noticed some old habits returning lately. I'm actually falling into the energy of 'please take care of me,'" I interrupted.

"I was picking that up" she added with satisfaction in her voice. "Cut the old energy loose. Tell yourself 'Fulvio, your energy is triggering me, but I won't follow those paths. I choose independence" she advised. " Dependency is a natural emotional state during childhood when unconsciously overprotective parents do everything to make you dependent on them. We are, therefore, dependent on them not only for our physical care but also for emotional support. This is normal but should stay in childhood. Staying in a deep state of dependency as an adult is due to your lack of equilibrium."

"When Fulvio found me, I was in a state of equilibrium. It was actually that energy that drew him to me. So why am I losing it now?"

"Try to internalize that you are flowing on an energy of falling in love and anticipating joy. It is a strong and, if you allow yourself to use it, very uplifting energy. You know that you will feel joy no matter what happens when you meet again. You haven't felt this way with any other man."

I had nothing to add. I knew that I didn't really want to be with a controlling man who would demand an accounting of every minute of my life because I'd already had that.

Julia started a list:

BALANCE
BEING FREE IN A RELATIONSHIP
PLAY
JOY
TAKING CARE OF YOUR OWN AFFAIRS
COMMUNITY
FEELINGS
GOODNESS

"His - hey sweety" I added.

"Hey, sweety. That's a good one!" she repeats happily. "Don't be afraid. Follow that thread. You're getting the most wonderful gift from life: the opportunity to experience falling in love. It's lovely, no matter how it ends."

"I also wanted to tell you that today I thanked my ex for leaving me" I told her. "I went to the office where we still work together and knocked on his door. I heard a cold 'come in' from inside. I went in. He was sitting at his desk with his current girlfriend. 'Forgive me, but I have to do this,' I said. Then I leaned over him, kissed him on the cheek, and said, 'Thank you so much for leaving. I would have never had the courage to do it." I was touched when I said this to him, and I felt such warmth and peace" I said.

Julia stayed silent for a moment, then she took a deep breath and said these beautiful words:

"You're amazing! This is the highest form of respect and gratitude one person can give another. Just one thing, dear. You say that Fulvio rarely writes to you and that you barely talk. There is no precise number of texts a man has to send if he loves you and cares about you. Enjoy this. Embrace it. Allow yourself to feel what you feel! Remember. You can spend two hours in bed with a man and not be as satisfied with him as with another man you spent five minutes with. Time is relative."

"You're right" I commented. "I wish I had a video of the whole thing. What I experienced lying next to him in bed was cosmic. Fulvio represents the epitome of beauty in my eyes. His face... even when he doesn't smile... but I can't handle it when he smiles. It's not a superficial beauty. There is something deeper in it. When I look into his loving and warm eyes and see his sincere and tender smile, I feel like I'm in paradise. His aura attracts me. When I am close to him, I feel peace, acceptance, and security... I feel bliss."

"I'm getting that from you" she says. "I'd love to hug you because you seem light as a feather, so soft and sweet. I always say that first blushes of love look like pink candy" she adds.

"Yes. That's me and Fulvio. Just my skin, those cuddles, that silence, that peace, that harmony - I don't need anything else to be happy. No pressure, no expectations, just reveling in our closeness... Thank you, Julia. Thank you for those miraculous words. This trip really is the greatest gift."

"Embrace this. Allow yourself to have it. Enjoy the hours that you spent with him. Be joyful that you got to feast your eyes and feed your senses. This is another great gift life is giving to you" Julia said. "You've never looked at a man this way before" she added tenderly.

She wrapped our session with these words:

"Remember, my love, that you have come a long way. You have already worked through many things, and you deserve to be surrounded by considerate people who love and respect you. This is wonderful, Iwona."

The lesson I learned is: Allow yourself to accept uncertainty.

The lesson you learned is:

Sailing

First conversation with my Italian lover on FaceTime.

How did this happen?

Friday. The familiar and long-awaited signal from WhatsApp. I grabbed the phone and… Yes! It's him! He wrote!

I quickly unlocked the screen and read:

"Hello, my sweet, how are you feeling?"

Should I write a text back or send a voice message? I'll record a message.

Hello. You ask me how I'm feeling. That's a complex matter at the moment. I get a little sad every evening when I'm home alone. I just finished my ceramics workshop. I like ceramics, and I like being with people who appreciate art. We talk, laugh and have a great time, but after two hours I have to go home... and that's not easy. I'd like to see you on video. I'd love it if you'd like that too. Lots of kisses and warm hugs for you, my handsome man.

A text comes back:

"Thank you, my sweet. How would you feel about a meeting on FaceTime tomorrow morning?"

"Siii."

We meet early on Saturday morning, starting our first videochat at 8 am, with him greeting me as follows:

"You look sexy and sweet even on phone screen. I miss you. I feel your absence here."

Once again, I could look deep into his eyes, be fed by the sound of his voice, and know that I'm not alone. It made me feel a mixture of excitement and embarrassment. Embarrassment? It surprised me too. Fulvio made me feel abashed like no other man. All my previously rebuilt self-confidence vanished like the last gust of the Italian summer.

That Sunday, I planned to visit my mother. Every time I visit her, I stop by the Gdansk Old Town, which I find to be the most architecturally beautiful place in Poland. And no matter how often I come here, I always feel the same emotion and enchantment.

That's my city!

I daydream about a walk with Fulvio. We walk along the cobblestone streets surrounded by thousands of tourists, inhaling the scents of the seaport and cotton candy. While waiting to cross the drawbridge, we admire the old granary and beautifully renovated houses. The water, in which the almost setting sun sparkles, breaks its delicate waves against the marina docks.

Gdańsk is the Polish city I love as profoundly as the Italian Florence, Bologna, and San Gimignano. And I am sure my feelings would be even more intense if I were here wrapped in my beloved's arms and I could watch the setting sun reflect in his eyes.

I sent Fulvio a few photos and an invitation to visit Gdańsk. In return, I received these sweet words:

"With you, any place will be magical."

And that's how Gdańsk became the first Polish city marked on the map of our dreams.

* * *

I returned to my home in Warsaw. I was greeted by one of those precious evenings when I received something more than just "Buona notte" from my Sicilian:

"I want you."

"I want you too."

I send him a photo of my black lace lingerie.

"That's so hot. Please let me see it on you."

"Right away or can you wait until you visit Warsaw?"

"I'd like to pick both."

"OK, but only if you promise to visit me as soon as possible."

"I promise."

"Not so fast. Please record your promise in a voice message."

"OK, recording."

I hear the recording:

Of course, honey. I promise I will come to Poland and stay there as long as I can, because I really need you.

This evening, you're super quick to respond to my messages - I joke in my own recording.

You don't like it? - he asks, laughing.

Of course, I like it. What are you doing right now?

I'm lying on the couch, listening to and reading your messages. Plus, I'm looking at photos of you, my sweet.

Let's meet at 9:39 pm - I propose.

Why exactly 39? - he asks with curiosity.

Because that's what I'd like. - I wrap our chat.

My beau doesn't know that at this moment, there's a purchase confirmation for a flight to Bologna in my Ryanair account.

How did I buy the ticket? - you ask.

I had a rough week. I developed intense anxiety, convincing myself that I would lose Fulvio and never see him again. So, without thinking much, I opened the flight calendar, and as soon as I saw a free Monday, I bought a ticket. The surge of emotions that enveloped me - exhilaration, euphoria, and heightened anticipation - rekindled cherished memories and ignited hope for reliving those treasured experiences.

"*What the heck*" I thought. "*Even if things don't work out with Fulvio, I will visit my sister. I love spending time with her.*"

I broke right away. Even though I didn't plan to, when I saw his smile and those wonderful eyes on our video chat, I told him about the ticket right away. His reaction was like a beautiful rainbow after spring rain.

"Did you buy a ticket?" He asked.

"Yes, I bought it."

"I'm so happy! This is the best birthday gift I could have dreamed of."

"Birthday?" I asked.

"Yes. October twenty-eighth is my birthday. No one has ever given me such a wonderful surprise."

"This is an incredible coincidence" I comment, "because this trip is also my birthday present to myself."

"Really? You're not kidding?" he asked.

"Not kidding. My birthday is just a few days after yours. This should be a great time for us both!"

"Thank you so much for doing this" he concluded.

* * *

Our first morning online sex date filled me with feminine energy again. I felt playful and lighthearted. Our evening doses of tenderness reignited me. I was surprised to see how little I needed to feel like I was surfing a wave of love and feel the wind in my hair.

In the morning, I put on a great outfit, my favorite high heels, and went to the office. I felt like I was floating. Surely, my aura was palpable to everyone around me. I stood out to everyone. My smile made some people happy too and put them in a good mood, while others were puzzled. I imagined each passer-by asking me in disbelief: "Hey, blondie! How can you be so happy at 8:00 am on a Monday?"

My great mood lasted all day. I felt loved, important, and needed again. It's interesting how quickly our perception of ourselves can change. Before I met Fulvio, I was sure that I was a completed project. I loved myself and believed that no one and nothing could shake my self-esteem. My charming Italian quickly showed me that it only seemed so to me. I realized that I still had a lot of work to do on myself.

All it took was for the man I cared about to not show me affection in exactly the way I expected, and my self-confidence plummeted. "Old demons" crept out of my attic. My arch enemy – Fear – was growing more potent, and I panicked and didn't know what to do with myself. I felt as if my world could collapse at any moment, something that I was unfortunately to experience that very evening.

At 9:02 p.m., inspired by our morning online play, I sent a cheeky:

"Hi, you up?" – … and I didn't get an answer.

What did I feel?

Anger at being ignored, disappointment at unfulfilled expectations, and disappointment at dashed dreams.

Why do we need the acceptance of others so much?

Why do we need love and recognition from other people so much?

Why do we look to others to fill our inner emptiness? Why can't we soothe ourselves?

Because no one ever taught us.

No one ever taught us that everything we ever need is within ourselves.

Instead, we were taught to search for our better half - to search in others for what we're missing.

The following morning, I no longer felt angry, but I didn't want to be on the losing end, so I decided to stay silent until he reached out to me. He could wait and wait. It was as if I were a little girl taking revenge on my parents for not doing what I wanted. But while this tactic will work with a child and devoted parents who will do everything to make their little princess happy, the effect on an independent man might be different.

And now I was asking myself: who is making who wait? I was not writing to him, because I was waiting for him to write first. It was still me waiting!

Falling in love with Fulvio made me realize that we only get to know ourselves fully through relationships with other people. We can tell ourselves that we are fully realized, feel great in our own company, are strong internally, and that nothing can throw us off balance. We may also think that we know everything about ourselves. However, only when fate puts another person in our path can we test ourselves and see how much of what we think is true and how much is just our imagination.

The more emotions your relationship with another person involves, the more it influences you and shows you the areas of yourself you need to work on. Looking into another person's eyes, you can see your own desires, fears and limitations.

After all that, at 6:31 am I saw a demure message that seemed to have a hint of remorse.

"Good morning my sweet, did you sleep well?"

"No, I did not. There were no messages, no news from you last night."

He sent a voice recording in response.

"I'm so sorry. I had a long and challenging day, but please don't stress. Everything is fine. I'm really sorry" - he spoke, sounding as if he was comforting and reassuring himself."

Perhaps because he was feeling guilty, or perhaps because he was feeling something else, Fulvio sent me a photo of himself before leaving for work.

During the day, unlike before, he messaged me to ask how I was feeling. In the evening - for the first time since we parted at the airport in Bologna - we messaged back and forth for almost three hours.

The next Friday morning, Fulvio, in a great mood and full of tenderness, informed me that he was going to visit his son, to Milan. I didn't think too much about this because I also visit my son often; no big deal. However, reality soon gave me an unpleasant check.

Fulvio disappeared behind Milan's city gates. The energy of this city absorbed him and my wonder-boy sank like a proverbial stone into water. He didn't message me all Saturday or show signs of life on Sunday.

So what did I do?

I called up my own strength and decided to participate in the game of hide and seek. I disappeared, too.

A message arrived on Monday morning and broke through all of my ice.

"Good morning my sweet, did you forget about me?"

"Is he kidding?" - I thought. "Who is this guy? Not a peep out of him all weekend and he asks me if I forgot about him?"

"I didn't forget about you. Looks like you forgot about me. I'm still awaiting an answer to the question I asked you on Saturday."

"It's impossible for me to forget you. You're a part of me. Forgive me. I was tired after three very intense days, but everything is fine. I miss you very much. I want to have you here with me in my arms, and I want to make love to you. I shower you with sweet kisses and I miss you."

"Damn it!"– I thought. "Where is the line between a healthy man minding his own business and a man disrespecting you? Could someone answer this for me? How much further do I need to stretch and push beyond my boundaries to stay within the energy of falling in love? What else will I have to ignore?"

The following days passed lazily. Without any fireworks. Every day, he sent a "good morning" and "good night" as if we were an old married couple. The relationship felt like something that was not nothing but nothing that could be called something.

Until this evening, when I was stirred in the bathtub by the sound of WhatsApp and the following message:

> "I need your kisses, your skin, your body above mine, your breasts, your taste, all of you. I keep hearing the sound of your "go, go, go."

I was incapable of staying indifferent to such a declaration. That evening, we had our second Facetime sex date.

In the morning, I got up lazily. I was relaxed and happy. Still surfing the wave of yesterday's excitement, I took out beautiful black stockings finished with a lace ribbon, and a black lace garter belt. I also picked out black high heels and a new burgundy dress.

I love stockings. They are so feminine. Every time I put them on, I think about my mother. My mother, who carried herself pretty modestly to avoid making my father jealous, maintained her elegance by never giving up stockings. I loved watching how gracefully she put them on. First, she'd gently remove them from their packaging and unwind them on the bed like twisty streamers. Then, she'd carefully take each stocking and stretch it over both hands. Eventually, in one fluid motion so as not to tear them, she'd put her slender foot between her hands and into the stocking. From the feet, she slowly went up towards the ankles, her beautifully defined calves, and after a short stop at knee height, she ended this sensual, almost erotic journey on her shapely thighs. The culmination of this ceremony was the attaching of garter belt clasps. This seemingly simple activity causes considerable difficulties for many women. You need precision in collecting the right amount of material to fasten the capricious clasp.

A WOMAN – ONE GARTER BELT, TWO STOCKINGS, AND FOUR CLASPS – SENSUALITY

This image will remain in my memory forever and will always bring back warm memories of my mother, who, throughout her life, held back her wild, feminine energy out of fear of rejection. And that's why I'm grateful that I can own my femininity as something that complements me and gives me strength.

Mom, I love you, and I'm sad that we never had the opportunity to talk to each other, woman to woman, and friend to friend, but I'm sure you love me, and I'm always in your heart.

I had quite an intense day at work, which was interrupted by a familiar feeling: a slight tightness in my chest, difficulty in taking in air, and deep, laboured breathing combined with feeling uneasy. After a while, though, relief and the image of Fulvio appeared before my eyes.

I wrote to him:

"My love. Who could be thinking about me so intensely that I'm losing concentration?"

I believe that when you think about a man, he is actually thinking about you. You are just sensing it.

After feeling like this, it is difficult to return to work as if nothing had happened. How can I stop the butterflies raging in my stomach, at least for a moment? Maybe it would be better not to fight it but just surrender to the feeling? I decided to observe myself and see where these emotions would take me.

I take a look at myself and see: dress, high heels, stockings...

"*Qualcosa di caldo?*[1]"

[1] Translation: Something hot?

"? ?"

"Will you write me something hot?
Is this a proposition?"

"Maybe."

"Wow, interesting."

"But I'm not a good writer."

"Maybe you can tell me a little something?"

"Pardon me, but my English and my Italian are rather weak."

"Maybe you can send me a picture?"

I send him a sensual photo of my calf wrapped in an elegant black stocking.

"Where are you?"

"At the office."

"Maybe something a bit more spicy?"

"Very, very spicy?"

"Yes, yes!"

I feel his euphoria. This time, he gets to see not only my calf but also my thigh, surrounded by the intricately woven lace that ends my stocking.

"Is that enough?"

"With you, I can't ever get enough. More please."

"That's impossible at the office. There are too many handsome men wandering about."

"Nooo, please."

"You're not busy?"

"I'm at home. Please…"

The third photo is of slender thighs in beautiful lace stockings and two clasps shyly peaking out from under the dress.

"If you want to see more, come over."

"Wow! You're wearing this at work? You're making me hot. I want you."

"Yes. I love stockings so every Autumn, I take them out of the drawer, stretch them over my hands, and delicately slide them onto my legs."

"Mmmmmm. I'm jealous."

"I hope so. ☺"

"I am! Please, send me one more photo."

I feel a hint of uncertainty creeping through my mind. Do it or let it go? Set sail on the ocean of unlimited fantasy or stay on the shore? I'm sailing. I won't be afraid anymore!

I step into the president's office, close the door, and pull up my dress to see my sun-kissed thighs next to the lace garter belt and, above them, lace black panties, emphasizing my narrow waist.

"Will that suffice?"

"No. Nothing is ever enough. It would be magical to have you here."

Another day at the office and I can't work. I feel excitement and slight fear. I don't know what comes first - whether my breathing speeds up and then my heart starts beating faster, or vice versa. A huge flock of butterflies wakes up in my stomach. There are so many of them that when they take off, they also lift my body. They slowly gain height, flapping their delicate wings. I feel them in my waist, chest and then in my throat. I can not concentrate. Numbers in Excel merge into a blur. I try to distract myself. I gather my thoughts to no avail. I try to take a few deep breaths... but it doesn't help. I'm still in that intoxication of love that comes out of nowhere, lasts a moment or two, and then goes away.

Suddenly, a question speeds across my mind, fast as a Cupid's arrow.

"Why don't you want to feel it?"

And then another.

"Why do you want to stop it? Why do you begrudge yourself something people wait years for, hoping it will happen to them?"

Feeling love, this purest form of energy is a true gift. When you are in it, you are overwhelmed by openness and selflessness. Love can equip us to look at others without judgment. Wouldn't it be better for us to live without manipulating other people?

"Blind love?" You ask.

No, love is not blind. This feeling allows you to see everything in another person, all that he has and often hides from the world because he either does not dare to show it or is unaware of his depth. Love for another person allows you to notice and approach their deficits with tenderness.

As Victor Hugo wrote in Les Miserables: “If we would take but little pains, the nettle would be useful; we neglect it, and it becomes harmful. Then we kill it. How much men are like the nettle!” Then he added “My friends, remember this, that there are no weeds, and no worthless men, there are only bad farmers.”[1]

“Maybe it’s not easy, but please, enjoy this” I whispered to myself. “Stay in this as long as you can. Find out what it can bring you, where it can take you, and how it can change your outlook and thinking. Allow yourself to consciously experience love.”

---

[1] Victor Hugo, Les Miserables.

The lesson I learned is: Giving into feeling is worth it.

The lesson you learned is:

I'm Scared

I've been crying all day today. I'm leaving you this voice message because I need to know: Am I expecting too much from a guy who says he needs me and that I'm important to him? 

These are the words that begin my message to Julia.

Am I asking too much by sending one short message a day and hoping that he will respond?

I don't know if this is a test of my strength or if we're just not right for each other?

I do not know what I should do?! I don't know if I understand this?! Or maybe I don't understand anything?!

My defense system immediately kicks in when Fulvio goes into sporadic contact mode. I think to myself: I'm going to get mad at him. I will treat him the same way he treats me. I'll ice him out like a teenager might their parent.

What should I do to find a more even keel? How do I maintain a relationship without clinging to a man and simultaneously cultivate what's sweet between us?

How can you find the balance between prioritizing and taking care of yourself and the madness of falling in love, which demands more and more?

How can you balance a sense of your own freedom and independence with needing to be with a man?

My dear, it has occurred to me that it would be simpler to fall out of love. Finding a few, or maybe a dozen, flaws in Fulvio would be much easier. I know because I'm a perfectionist at it. I wouldn't need much time. I'm an expert at taking offense. I took my lessons from the greatest master I knew - my father, who would not speak to my mother for several days to punish her for any disobedience. Taking offense is what I do best.

After a breakup, I could tap into the feeling of being offended at my needs not being met. I could use that feeling to work on myself and build my independce. I could easily pretend again that I have already worked through all of my issues, that there are no old skeltons in my closet. I could explain my failures by saying that I meet the wrong men. I wouldn't have to challenge myself or waste time analyzing my reactions and what triggers them and why. Why do I feel ignored when I don't get what I want?

Why do I think that a person who does not anticipate my every need, does not respect me?

Why, despite my fifty-four years of age, do I pout in silence like a little girl when I want to get back at someone?

I finished the recording and started crying again.

"This can't be the way!" – I thought. "I don't want to act like I used to."

I want to be:

- busy with my own affairs, but not selfish;
- independent but not inaccessible;
- strong but not domineering;
- balanced but not cold;
- self-loving but not selfish;
- free but not lonely.

I really struggle. Sometimes I feel anxious several times a day. I get overwhelmed by a sense of resignation.

I don't know if I did the right thing when I decided once again not to write to Fulvio.

I don't know who I want to punish and for what.

Him for not meeting my expectations, or myself for getting myself into such a situation? Time will tell.

FEAR IS AN ENERGY – A COMMON PART OF EVERY PERSON

The weekend was coming up. So I wrote to my Sicilian that I hoped his next trip to Milan would not be like the last one. He ignored it. He didn't reply, he didn't react and I heard nothing from him for two days. This was already becoming a weekend tradition.

Less than a year ago, I would have given it all up. I would get offended and find someone else.

But not now. Why not now?

Because I want to learn as many lessons as possible from being with Fulvio! I want to grow.

Our relationship is akin to a "conscious relationship" - a concept described by therapists as a relationship where both partners purse a commitment to growth.

Bartek Stefański, a great Polish therapist, once wrote on his FB page:

> "A conscious relationship shows you where you really are. If deep down you feel lonely, a relationship will make you feel even more lonely. If you are afraid of commitment deep down, the relationship will increase your fear of the unbearable. It's not because you're suffering. It's because the universe is trying to heal you. This is your wake-up call.

> This is the great paradox of relationships. We believe they can soothe our wounds or fill our void. Still, ultimately – especially in a sacred relationship – your wounds and emptiness will be magnified and exposed even more.
>
> This is why many people become independent or claim to be 'free spirits,' but deep down, they are simply too afraid to face the severity of their trauma and pain. Relationships are not here to reassure you or make you comfortable. They are there to wake you up and end your cyclical suffering. They are your wake-up call."[1]

These are strong words whose meaning I discovered when I started therapy. I believe in them.

I believe there is a reason why life put an Italian with a hypnotic smile and an intoxicating look in my path. A man who affects me so much that I can't even be angry with him.

Thanks to Fulvio, I realized that I had never been with a man whose financial status I was not interested in. I was always subconsciously looking for a partner who could bring me some form of safety, who could provide me with a comfortable life. Someone I could anchor myself to for a long, predictable life.

And now?

For some reason, I am not attracted to Karol - an entrepreneur who is interested in me and could give me the proverbial stars from the sky. Who has a beautiful house surrounded by a forest and a thriving business. With whom I could go skiing in the winter and spend a wonderful time by the water in the summer.

If I wanted to, I could live peacefully with him. I would have what I once dreamed of. Certainly, over time, I would get involved in his businesses, which would make me feel that I was important and needed.

---

[1] Translated from original Polish. Find Bartek Stefanski's page (https://bartekwstefanski.pl/)

I would be a helper to him and… I'd repeat the same role I played with my ex.

It is easy for me to give up my life and my needs to devote myself to others - even if they don't ask for it. I realized that a relationship with Karol could be a return to the past. If I hadn't, I would have slipped into my old world.

Maybe the fact that - despite all the advantages that Karol has - I only like him is my subconscious defense strategy? Perhaps the universe is protecting me from stepping in the same quicksand twice?

I know it is second nature for me to lose myself and give up everything that is mine, even when no one asks me to do so.

It may seem unlikely, but if I hadn't met Fulvio and Karol, I wouldn't have uncovered that despite undergoing therapy and working on myself, I still have this tendency to give up on myself. In this way, I could give up on many dreams, like having my own company, publishing a book, and living independently.

Maybe that's the reason I'm drawn to Fulvio? To an office worker who has to ask for every day of leave, lives in a company apartment, drives a company car, and dresses in sneakers and a sweatshirt?

But why am I so drawn to him? Why did I fall in love with him?

Why is he the only man I want to be with?

Yet again, I have to confess that I'm uncertain about what to think or how to act.

In the stillness of the night, I try to soothe the chaos swirling in my mind, desperately seeking a semblance of order amidst the emotional storm. Yet, the answers remain elusive, just out of reach. Even with the miles I've traveled on this journey of self-discovery, I'm still lost in a darkness of uncertainty. My mind insists, "Leave him; he's not worth it." But my heart aches for the warmth of his smile, the intensity of his gaze, and the irresistible pull of his energy. And then there's my soul, tempting me with a tantalizing promise, "Take the leap, and you'll discover wonders beyond your wildest dreams."

I thought that a soothing bath was the only thing that might help my current state. I filled the spacious, three-person bathtub with warm water. I infused the bubble bath with a few drops of fragrant orange oil and turned on my favorite music.

I immersed myself in pleasantly warm and relaxing water, spread a wonderfully creamy bath gel on a soft, milky foam sponge and with gentle, circular movements massaging my entire body, I removed the day's dust. After a while, I had the impression that I was washing away something more, that I was cleansing more than just my body. Nostalgia flooded in, followed by the well-known feelings of falling in love, understanding and love.

I started to cry.

I picked up my phone. In the photo gallery I found the one phone of Fulvio and I standing next to each other at the airport. I looked at my handsome man and tears welled up in my eyes. I couldn't - I didn't want to stop it anymore. With tears, I slowly released the emotions of sadness and longing for what I missed.

I looked into my Sicilian's eyes and asked:

"Tell me, my love, what is it about you that makes me so drawn to you?" And I enlarged his photo.

And then I knew!

Those black eyes, full of love and warmth, were like a drug to me. Another wave of tears spilled from my blue eyes, followed by joyful laughter.

Yes. I cried and laughed for a few minutes. As if I was happy to meet someone I hadn't seen for a long time. As if I had regained someone close to me.

A friend? An old lover?

I tired myself out with all this laughing and crying and I went to bed. I fell asleep.

* * *

"Fulvio is not some random man, he's once in a lifetime." Is how I began next session with Julia. How do I know this? Because he's the only one that makes me react so intensely. I met three men after my breakup. In their company I felt balanced and strongly grounded in my femininity. I spoke clearly about my needs, what I like and dislike. I felt free from expectations, I was minding my own business and living in harmony.

None of these men showed me a path towards growth. None of them challenged me. Even though I enjoyed spending my free time with them and quite liked them, I couldn't fall in love with any of them.

I tried to make myself. I couldn't.

Look what's happening with Fulvio! He destroys me! On Sunday, I spent the whole afternoon sobbing into my pillow again. I have moments when anxiety suddenly tightens my chest and throat, I have difficulty catching a breath, and I panic in search of something to do to relieve my stress. I know that my Italian lover has something to teach me, but how should I interpret this lesson and protect my sanity?!"

I finished my long monologue and Julia spoke.

"My dear, Fulvio affects you differently than other men, because not only do you like him very much, but you also fell in love with him. Of course you didn't plan for it. It just happened and you had no choice. The experience was sent to you for a reason. Now, please look within, what image does the idea of love bring up for you? What type of energy do you associate with it? When you think: 'I love Fulvio,' what do you feel other than butterflies in your stomach, euphoria and elation?"

"The first thing that comes to my mind is the fear of losing him" I answer.

"Exactly!" Julia reacts like a teacher hearing a great answer from a student. "For you, love and the fear of losing it are inseparable. Your parents showed you this pattern. They were anxious, living in eternal fear for you and encoded this mechanism. You lived in a controlling household where your mom and dad saw danger everywhere and repeated:

'We love you, that's why we are afraid for your health. We love you, that's why we fear for your life. We love you, that's why we're afraid for you. We're afraid, we're afraid, we're afraid…'"

LOVE AND FEAR.
ARE THEY AN INSEPARABLE TOXIC DUO?

"Fear is energy and like any other energy it comes to you unexpectedly" Julia continues. "For you, my dear, fear appears because you are afraid of losing love. When you become aware of feeling love, one step behind it, like a twin brother, is your fear of losing."

"That's right" I interjected. "Yesterday I did a stream of consciousness writing session just to face this fear. I asked myself what I was afraid of, and look what I wrote:

I'm afraid that he doesn't love me.

I'm afraid that I will never see him again.

I'm afraid that he will never hug me again and I won't be able to feel the way I felt when we were together."

"What brings up your fear are the words: "I AM AFRAID" my therapist replied. "Our culture teaches women to be afraid. We hear: 'aren't you scared something could happen?' or 'oh no, I can't do that, I'm too afraid.'

What you are doing is called building relationships based on fear of loss and rejection. The only love you know is love with fear. You're unaware that by using the words "I am afraid", you are inviting fear into your space. That word is a key.

Therefore, if fear appears, you must understand that it's only the creation of your mind and you cannot allow yourself to give in to it. Don't feed fear, when you give into it you feed it and make it grow. Take some deep breaths and say to fear, 'I see you, but I do not nourish you.' Then your fear won't be a part of you, but something outside.

You've banished fear from within you, but he would like to come back in and control you again. So it circles around you and slips through from time to time to feed. If you know that you have already gotten rid of it once, you should know that you do not need to feed it anymore. For you, to love means being to be afraid of rejection and loss. It's like your personal love code. You're far from the only only who struggles with this. You can change your thinking. Fear is and will always accompany us in some respect, because it is one of our primal energies, but it is up to us whether we let it carry us away. One thing you can do is literally rephrase which words and ideas you allow into your thoughts. Take the edge out.

For example, replace: 'I'm afraid that I will never see him again,' with 'I'd love to see him again.' 'I'm afraid that I'll lose him,' with 'I'd like to hug him again.' Replace 'I'm afraid he'll leave me, ' with 'I miss him.'

We got some beautiful insights today. Fear is a living energy that circulates the earth. It just is. Keep trusting that life is leading you places for a reason: for adventure, for love, for experience. Trust that this process is guiding you properly. Trust the tide, trust the force of life that leads to good places. Throw off your masks and face the naked truth of yourself. THIS IS HOW I AM. No pretense."

"I wrote a letter to my dad" I told her. "I wrote about all of my pain, unfulfilled expectations, lack of love and loneliness that I felt as a child. I had thought that I'd dealt with all of this a long time ago and I was sure that my heart was free from it. I wrote it and after a few days I decided to burn it. The last time I read this letter, I took some matches and went to the bathroom. I lit one corner of the paper and looking into the flame, I began speaking to the spirit of my departed father.

I was crying and said: "I miss you so much my beloved papa. I love you so much and I wish you were here. I know you loved me too. You just didn't always know how to show it. I know that you're proud of me. I love you."

That process made me feel clearer and lighter. Then ten minutes later, Fulvio had called me. It was mystical. You know what else? When I burned this letter, I also let go of all my anger towards Fulvio, and all men. I thought about fully respecting them as individuals. For the first time, I really focused on the idea of men as full beings with rights.

The right to be human.

The right to be imperfect.

The right to weakness.

The right to freedom.

The right to everything I haven't given them the right to previously.

I grew up in a family where relationships were so stilted that men were seen as a means to an end. Women, as if in revenge for being mistreated for generations, refused to respect the men. They openly resented them. They voiced it at family meetings. I heard degrading pronouncements spoken out loud like 'You're stupid;' 'Why don't you make yourself useful?; 'You're a drunk,' or 'Why don't you do something helpful instead of hanging about!" It was normal for our family meetings to turn into trading complaints about which of my uncles or my father did something wrong or did not do something they should have. I'd hear; 'A man's job is to make money for the family. He must be a provider. He must be tough and strong. Real men are not soft. Real men have balls.'

It wasn't just my family who saw them like this, it was a common attitude. I often had the impression that if women didn't need men to support the family, they would have gotten rid of them a long time ago. The only thing that kept a woman in the marriage was the fear of not being able to cope on her own.

Just as men did not ask women, women dancing this toxic social dance did not ask men about their needs, emotions, and problems. To relieve their pain and anesthetize themselves, Polish men took the only cure available on a limited budget... Alcohol, which, ironically, was always available even in very difficult times when food was scarce, including during martial law. Unfortunately, the cure was killing the patient. Alcohol insulated a man from emotions and gave him a sense of carefreeness, but it was addictive. So men needed more and more of it to change their real world into the one they dreamed of. This just added fuel to the spiral of separation from family life, and pushed them to the periphery where they stayed as losers and drunkards."

"Well, we went deep! Thank you for this evening!" I told Julia at the end of our session.

* * *

In the morning, I was once again visited by Fear. This time he adopted a different tactic. He sat on my shoulder and promised that as soon as I ended my relationship with the Italian, he would leave for good.

"An offer I can't refuse" I said ironically.

Actually, it would be a way to resolve this- leave the guy before he leaves me. Just in case. Be the first. Better to abandon someone out of fear than to be abandoned.

I think about a Dale Carnegie quote I once read. "Do the thing you fear to do and keep on doing it… that is the quickest and surest way ever yet discovered to conquer a fear."

"Don't even think that I'm going to give up on being in love" I tell Fear. "I have time, so I can just wait to see what fate brings me. I don't care what happens. If Fulvio doesn't want to be with me, he'll leave. I know how I feel about him, and I'm not interested in what you, Fear, think or plan. I am in love and I feel great about being in love. I won't end it just to avoid something that scares me. As my therapist Julia says: 'Love finds a way. If one ends, another appears.'"

I know Fear's tactics very well. When he's done with one topic, he immediately clings to the next worry. In my case, there are too many to pick from. Publishing a book, starting a new company, my current job and a million other things to be afraid of. Fear doesn't know though that I would rather experience the pain of failure than be afraid and do nothing. I choose action regardless of the consequences. If I fall, so be it.

The lesson I learned is: You can defeat fear if you're courageous.

The lesson you learned is:

Waking Up

I take pottery classes, it's like a return to my childhood. I remember how much I liked art and shop classes in school. I also remember how much I loved learning embroidery and crocheting from my mother. Those were past times that helped me get out of my head and stop overthinking.

I found Barb's art studio right after the separation with my ex. The workshops were like a lifeline thrown to me by fate. Here I met women with a passion for painting, sculpting, crocheting and more

Today is another workshop Friday. However, I no longer want to paint a picture of an iris. I don't have a heart for it anymore. Now I have the urge to sink my fingers into clay and sculpt.

I get an idea - inspired by my current heart entanglement with a motorcycle enthusiast - to sculpt an angel sitting on a bike. Unfortunately, to get from the stage of "I have an idea" to "I have a sculpture of an angel sitting on a bike" you have to travel through a creative process.

I'm forced to very quickly realize that my process may not be creative enough. My hands and my imagination don't want to cooperate, and the clay is too soft to play the role of peace broker. Still, I persist, and after two hours, a wonderful, golden-brown, angelic boy with a mohawk hairdo emerges from my "magical" hands. He has a red electric guitar slung over his shoulder and a red and gold "peace and love" badge on his chest. Unfortunately, he's not on a motorbike, but he still reminded me of Fulvio, because I gave him a slouchy posture just like his.

The best thing about these art workshops is that I'm not forced to do anything. I'm allowed to do what I feel.

I'm having an awakening and that applies to the business sphere too. I've just spent a busy weekend with Aldona, my web designer friend, working on the site for IMONA, a company I head with a business partner.

What's an IMONA? It's a composite. I like Iwona, my name. M for Monika, the name of my business parter. ONA means HER in Polish, that's who our clients are - business women. Passionate women full of vision and ideas.

Our client is an owner of a company who is overwhelmed or even annoyed by the mess of business administration. She hates paperwork, but by law, she must maintain paper copies of key documents. She dreams about going to the office and having all of these files magically organized, stored and labeled. Our company will create these and other miracles.

I am - just like my clients - a business owner, a woman, a mother... which allows me to empathize with their needs and problems.

I had been a "great woman behind a great man" for many years. So how did I get the guts to start my own company after so many years of running a business with my ex? Well, maybe not entirely my own because I have a wonderful partner, but the word "own" is very meaningful to me because it means that my ex is not in it.

It all started seven years ago when I met a woman with such a sweet soul that even when she swore, the words took on songbirds' bright and beautiful sound. I found myself in London and needed a place to stay. My ex-boyfriend helped me as he is a great people-connector. 'Stay with us,' he said, and that's how I met his girlfriend Margaret. Our paths crossed again in March of this year when she became my coach and saved me after a breakup. (But that's a story for another book. Ha ha!)

Thanks to Margaret, I met Marta - an angel of a woman who teaches people to live in lightness and the now, and who invited me to attend an anniversary meeting of her "School of Women Leaders." I went, even though I had no business being there since it was an event only for former workshop participants.

It was a wonderful June afternoon. I was waiting for Marta at "Frida" restaurant.

I really felt a need to be in community with other women. Although I had already overcome a sharp turn in my life's path, ahead, I still saw nothing. That evening I met many women full of happiness, creativity and courage. We talked about business and life, while enjoying the restaurant's incredible food. I started with margarita and shrimp in a spicy sauce. I didn't notice when Monika sat down next to me but then something sparked between us quickly. Around 10 p.m. we had already developed a plan for a joint business. Two weeks later we founded the company. That evening, I received a book from the event's organizer with the following dedication: "Be afraid. Do it anyway."

TWO WOMEN - ONE EVENING - IMONA

At the first meeting with Aldona, a design expert beyond just website construction, we developed a company logo, business cards and an advertising slogan.

The previous evening, we attended a Gabrielle Roth 5Rhythms, dynamic movement class, had a delicious dinner at an Italian food restaurant, and ended the night in the same bed. (Ha ha! We crashed, tired.) Then we ate breakfast got to work.

We both worked in our pajamas on the comfortable sofa. Total freedom, open minds, my heart in a state of love, and we were in a state of flow.

Fulvio, despite it being the weekend, contacts me. He records a short message about how lonely he is and how he misses me. I even feel a little sorry for him because he is sitting alone at home, in Bologna, under a torrential downpour, with no chance to go for a bike ride or a walk.

A moment later I get another message.

My Sweet. How are you feeling? It's still raining here, so it won't be a nice day, but I'm happy because it's one day closer to you visiting me. My precious.

How wonderful it is to be in love and make your dreams come true!

* * *

Big news. I'm allowing myself to hope and dream.

I've always been afraid to do it because I couldn't face the possibility of failure. I also preferred not to build my hopes up so as not to feel disappointed when they'd be dashed.

However, I recently attended a meeting of a "your 5-9 before the 9-5" club and it inspired me to think about possibilities. So I took out a red lipstick from my makeup bag and started creating my list of dreams. Today is the day when I will fulfill my dream number eleven.

"What dream is it?" You'll ask.

You might not believe it, but I'm doing a tandem sky dive today. I wouldn't believe it either, but I'm holding the printed invitation in my hand, and I'm already at the air base with my son.

Then it's my turn to go up. Dressed in a sky-diving jumpsuit and strapped into safety gear, I wait on the airport bench. A beautiful girl approached me. She has gorgeous red curls that bounce like springs in the wind, sweet freckles, and a luminous smile.

"Hey, call me Squirrel" she tells me. "I'll be recording your jump. What's the occasion?"

"I'm celebrating turning fifty" I tell her with a smile.

"I wouldn't have guessed you're fifty" she comments.

"Well, I'm celebrating turning fifty, but about four years too late" I smile and close my eyes, and then we both burst into laughter. "I was supposed to do this four years ago."

"So what happened?" My videographer inquires, intrigued.

"A certain person scared me away from it and I gave up. When I broke up with that person, I decided that the first thing I would do was jump! Ha, ha, ha!" We both break into big, belly laughter.

Squirrel extends her arm towards me and offers a high-five. I take her up on it with pleasure.

"Fantastic! Awesome! You'll see, it'll be amazing." She encourages me, and I give her a thumbs up in thanks.

A short walk across the green grass of the airport to the small plane. Me, a smiling blonde with carefully braided ponytails, and on either side of me walk my partners: Wiewióra, who is as cheerful and as excited as I am, and very nice and cheerful Marcin the instructor I'll be jumping with.

Our plane slowly climbs to thirteen thousand feet. In addition to me, four other pairs of skydivers and two extreme free-flight enthusiasts are on the plane. Before the jump, we all greet each other by touching each other's hands in a way typical of the SkyDive club.

We sit on the edge of the plane. Me and Marcin, to whom I am strapped. I feel so safe. There is endless open space in front of me. I don't feel afraid, although I've been terrified of open spaces all my life. Squirrel, standing by the plane's wall, looks at me with a smile. Marcin leans us back in order to throw us out of the plane with full force.

We're falling!

I feel like I'm on a rollercoaster. I realize that I have no control, but contrary to my norm, I'm able to put my complete trust in this moment. For the first time in my life, I feel completely still and unencumbered. There is only me and the falling.

Then the longest fifty seconds of my life, i.e. free-falling. I hear a roaring of noise. I feel joy when I spot Squirrel in front of me. She's not only feeling me but is feeling this joy too. My instructor decides to spin me around a bit. We make several revolutions around our own axis. I lose my bearings for a moment. The instructor signals that it's time to open the parachute. I give Squirrel a high five and then…

Silence.

I could stay here for the rest of my life and then one day longer - I think. I experience true silence for the first time ever. Real silence is not just the absence of sounds reaching you. When I feel it, it’s a full-body experience - silence in my ears, stillness in my mind, and peace in my heart.

In this blissful state we land in the grass of the airport. I’m at a loss for words. I’m still there, among clouds, birds and the great stillness.

Squirrel runs up to me and takes a few photos.

“This is the best thing I’ve ever done!” I say to her recording camera and let out a spontaneous exclamation. “Woooooo!!!!”

Later, I threw my arms around my instructor’s neck. I was so happy. Coming home, I felt like I was levitating. It was hard to be present in my body or in my car.

What did I do today? Today I used courage to make one of my deepest dreams come true.

Fulvio was impressed by my feat. He was very happy. At least until I sent him photos of me and my handsome jump instructor in an embrace. He texts:

“Hands off my sweetheart!”

Typical hound dog, I think. Doesn’t fully want me for himself, but doesn’t want anyone else to come hear me. Ha!

That evening, Fulvio sent me gorgeous videos from his motorcycle trips and his dives to explore shipwrecks.

I thought about how special it is that common interests can bring people together. It’s a gift. I got overwhelmed by emotions when I watched Fulvio's slideshow of the Campo Imperatore mountain meadowlands. Fulvio took beautiful photos and added captivating music. I was captivated by the breathtaking landscapes and faces of happy people he caught in the photo frame. Moments like this make life worth living.

I text:

"I'm looking forward to spending time with you, your friends and these beautiful places."

* * *

My new business, IMONA, came to life and brought with it new responsibilities, such as a photo session for our new website.

"This shoot is going to be awesome!" says our photographer, Julita. "I can already feel your energy. It will be a beautiful session and a beautiful website."

Each of us came to the session with a suitcase of clothes. Our company colors are powder pink, navy blue and white.

"Why a powder pink?" You might wonder.

When I got my own place after breaking up with my ex, I started a renovation. First I needed to organize things in my head, but after some time I also needed to organize my home space. I felt like I was getting rid of old energy with each changed item or colour. I painted the previously creamy-green walls white, bought luxe white bedspreads, and brought hand-crocheted lace tablecloths and napkins from my family home. I replaced some furniture and... Something else was missing. I went to the website of a popular store and saw a wonderful powder pink blanket. I fell in love. That evening, I placed an order for a blanket, pillow, and night lamps in that most female-coded colour - powder pink.

First, a hair and make-up session. Photo shoots have their own rules, after all.

Then, I stand in front of the camera. No big deal, just a few photos, you think, until you realize your photos will be sent out into the wide world.

Will I run away or break through my fear and brave this necessary task?

When you come face to face with the camera, there is nowhere to hide. The photographer can sense all of your emotions, even the deeply hidden ones. She senses my energy immediately. She smiles and takes me into a world of daydreams.

"For this photo, look directly at me but think about your man" she says. "Think about Fulvio and your first meeting. Your first walk together. Your first kiss."

With prompts like this, I could work for her all day.

"When you see your own photos, you inevitably spot what others do not see. Publishing pictures of yourself is a real exercise in letting go of perfectionism. It's never easy because you feel vulnerable and defenseless. Courage is very useful in such moments. I've heard it said that the greatest act of courage is being the hero of your own life.

I would say it a bit differently: "The biggest act of courage is to become the author of your own life."

* * *

Today I remembered a conversation with Julia. During one of our August sessions, I told her that life is wonderful, and the most wonderful thing is that every day I am curious about where I will be tomorrow. I also said that I was very curious about where I would be in December.

This is a huge change for me.

Previously I always looked into the future with fear and uncertainty. I preferred not to know what awaited me because I didn't expect anything good. After nine months of therapy and after consciously deciding to live in the energy of falling in love, I am curious who else the universe will put in my path, what plans it has for me and what else life will bring.

When I said these words in August, I didn't know yet that I would be writing a book. December has just begun, and I am absorbed in writing and discussing the process of publishing it with my manager, Michael.

I realize that it's been a long time since I planned the things that have happened in my life (except for buying tickets to Italy and skydiving). Being an active participant in my life feels like a great gift from fate.

Today I am curious where life will take me and where I will be next spring.

How far will I dare to swim out, how fully will I allow myself to wake up?

The lesson I learned is: There is nothing more important than creating your-self.

The lesson you learned is:

....
....
....
....
....
....
....
....
....
....
....
....
....
....
....
....
....
....
....
....
....
....
....
....
....
....
....
....

Shameless

“Why do you keep putting the breaks on what you feel for Fulvio?” Asks my therapist Julia.

“Because I don't want him to get bored with me” - I answer and hear her laughing. “My issue is that I can hear my mother and my aunt Mary in my head, calling me a shameless woman” I explain.

“Exactly! And what if it turns out that this man came along to let you express some shameless behaviour? We never know why we meet people at any given time” Julia explains.

These are the commandments I received from the women of my family:

“Remember, you can't ever show a man that you care about him!”

“Don’t chase after a guy because he won't respect you!”

“If you give a man everything he wants, he will get bored of you!”

“If you show him too much skin, he'll think you’re a slut.”

I never questioned where this wisdom came from. Who did they hear it from or when did they develop these beliefs? I know one thing. The fire of shameless femininity and sexuality has been lit within me, and the only man with whom this fire resonates is Fulvio.

* * *

I spent another morning surfing a wave of elation. I reach into the drawer with my sexy stockings and take a photo of them lying casually on my bed. I send it with the caption "TODAY IS STOCKINGS DAY."

Of course, my lover reacts right away.

"My love, you know that I love stockings so please don't forget to pack them when you visit. And one more thing. I love to see them anytime, but they look so much better when they're on your body and not on the bed."

I love his playfulness. I sent him a smiley face emoji and headed to the office.

Three weeks before my flight to Bologna I received another message.

"My love, I am waiting for you to be here."

"Dearest, we have three weeks to wait, which is both nothing and far too long."

That day, my Sicilian beau sent me a photo of himself on a motorbike, and in response I sent him a photo of us from the airport with the caption: "Sweet Memories".

As we got closer to my visit, my wonder-boy became more attentive. He wrote more often and longer, recorded sweet messages. It felt like he wasn't entirely sure I would come. This also invigorated my feelings. I felt loved again, and more sexy ideas played in my mind.

On Saturday, full of lovesick sighs and butterflies, I prepared a bath. I turned on some romantic music, turned on twinkle lights around the bathtub and took some romantic and suggestive photos. Surrounded by thick foam, in the twilight of the lights, I looked and felt very sensual and sexy. I sent him some of the photos with the caption:

"All of this is waiting for you, my love."

I love these evenings when, focused on love and trust, I stop to think about the gift that is my independent life. In those moments I feel truly grateful for every day, every minute of my new self.

I had no idea that I could ever be as happy and optimistic about my future as I am now, with so much going on. I have always preferred a stable life - a comfortable old armchair with a spring that cuts into my butt, rather than a new chair that requires me to give up old habits. I used to react to the word "change" with panic and defensiveness. I'd stick out my claws and get into attack mode in defense of the old order. Better the devil you know, right? This kind of fear kept me in my old relationship for so many years.

It is lovely how fast - thanks to therapy and fantastic people - I went through my transformation. I haven't looked back, and in my "new" life, I've rejected most superstitions and old beliefs.

Forgive me, grandmothers and mom, but I'm no longer interested in being a martyr who is waiting for eternal life. I do not agree to go through voluntary suffering just to reach some paradise gates one day.

Paradise is for everyone.

The Creator loves us all and doesn't want us to sacrifice ourselves. Mom, grandmother, dearest aunts and uncles. Members of my clan, forgive me, but I was not born to be a saint!

I do not agree with the restrictions that gender imposes on us. I do not agree that a woman is less than a man. I do not agree that in the 21st century, we should still be stuck with superstitions of the distant past.

Who created all these limiting expectations of women that we have been instilled since our childhood, and why? I have the suspicion that people created them in spite and jealousy, to make sure no one else could have a better life than them. The words of my grandmother are a great fit in this moment. I'd heard her say more than once, when she was feeling the hurt and and regret of a life she didn't have control over:

"I had suffered. Let other women suffer too" ... how sad it that, right?

I not only don't want to be a pious woman, I don't want to behave like a proper lady either. I want to be perceived as a human - a first and foremost a feeling, and then a thinking being.

On my way home from work I stop, as always, by my favorite park. I write to Fulvio:

"I am at the park and I want to tell you that I miss you. Your sweet kisses, the touch of your strong arms, your tenderness, and the ecstasy I felt when our bodies were so close. I have never felt like this with any man. When I looked deep in your eyes and our bodies were so tangled, I felt that I was alive. I miss talking to you, your brilliance, sense of humor and delicacy. You lit a fire in me. I want you to know that when we were together, I felt beautiful. You are important to me."

"I feel all of this too, my sweet. I miss you so much."

So, the winds of falling in love had reached Bologna. I wasn't surprised. Falling in love is a primal force, and if we let it embrace us it will do so immediately and with great pleasure. It would be wonderful if we could all give it up.

How beautiful and interesting would our lives be if we could look at other people with tenderness and appreciation for their imperfections.

When the finds of falling in love arrived in Bologna, a real love storm broke out in Warsaw. I dreamed of my Italian all night and the first thing I did as soon as I woke up was send him a message:

"I spent the night with you, my love."

"Good morning, my sweet. I want you."

"I want you too."

"Mmmm, please send me a spicy picture."

I'm in Warsaw, he is in Bologna. So far apart and yet so close. When love ignites the heart and soul, nothing can contain that fire.

I revealed my neckline and belly, and surreptitiously smuggled in a piece of lace underwear into the photo's frame.

"Your body is so beautiful, it sets me on fire, my love. I'm dreaming about being with you."

I run to the bedroom, I lie on the bed. I feel light and ethereal. The morning sun wraps my around my body. My partially closed eyes call out: "Come to me, come to me", and my parted lips shout: "I want you!" My body, still remembering the sun of southern Italy, longs for a moment of pleasure.

Rays of sun flit playfully across my ribs, which rise and fall evenly with my breathing. Their movement clearly harmonizes with the emotions I experience. My small breasts, firm like Sicilian oranges, wait eagerly for a lover.

I want you. I want to feel your body on my body. I want your taste. You make me insatiable - flows music from Bologna.

We start the dance of lovers.

Our video sex date is full of tender words, delicate touch and care for our shared intimacy. We enjoy what we can feel while waiting for the day we meet in person again. After the act of elation, we say goodbye to each other, wishing each other a wonderful day.

* * *

Friday evening. I sit on the living room, completely bathed in love. Hundreds of butterflies rush between my chest and throat as if they were taking part in a marathon. Their race grows in intensity every minute. I can not hold myself back.

I write:

"A few sweet kisses?"

The answer comes immediately, as if he'd been waiting for my message.

"Anywhere you'd like to have them, my sweet."

"First, I'd like one on my lips."

"And then?"

"The nape of my neck. A long and passionate kiss, please."

"Absolutely, my love."

"But that's not enough for me. Please do pay some attention to my breasts."

"Oooh, yes. Tell me, maybe your back and legs next?"

I'm sitting on the sofa in an evening dress. Why? I was invited to a party and right at this moment, I am trying on a dress that waited in the closet for seven years. Feeling full of feminine sexual energy, I send a photo of my bare legs wrapped only in flimsy chiffon. On my feet are delicate, satin high heels, black, which pair perfectly with the vivid red colour of my nails.

"You look so sexy in that dress. Wow. What's the occassion?"

"I'm going to a party."

"You'll be the most beautiful woman there. Don't forget that you're mine!"

"Yes, but none of that matters when I'm not with you."

A moment of silence and a question flies across the one thousand two hundred kilometers dividing Warsaw and Bologna.

"What??"

Just a small Whatsapp glitch. My answer arrived next to a different message than it was intended for, but still fits perfectly.

What happens when you devote yourself to the energy of falling in love is unbelievable. You get a kind of aura that works on everyone around you. Suddenly, strangers smile at you, doors open for you, and handsome strangers send you meaningful glances.

Every girl knows: when you have a man, that's the moment when everyone else want you.

I'm walking to the office. I teeter in high heels on a cobblestone sidewalk. James Brown gets in my head, singing "This is a man's world." If it was a woman's world, we would never have cobblestones. Ha ha.

"How are people supposed to walk on this in high heels?" I think.

I choose instead, to walk on the smoothly paved street. Drivers pass me and I see surprise on their face and questions in their expressions.

"What are you doing, woman?!"

"Where are you going, blondie?!"

Some drivers pass me calmly, others honk. Suddenly, one car stops. A handsome blond man lowers the window of his Mercedes, smiles at me, and explains that the road is for cars, not for pedestrians. With a big smile that matches his, I answer.

"Good morning! Nice to meet you! Yes, I know what the road is for, but have you ever tried to walk on a cobbled sidewalk in six-inch stilettos? Who had the brilliant idea to keep cobbled sidewalks? I am convinced it was a man because many women can't live without their heels. We're not in the ancient times when everyone walked around barefoot or in leather sandals, clothed in a piece of canvas."

I raise my leg slightly and show him my satin black boots.

"I respect that" he flirts.

"Thank you very much. I'm on a quest to make my life beautiful." I tell him.

He looks at me flirtatiously and smiles a gorgeous smile.

"Have a wonderful day. I hope we run into each other again" he says with unveiled hope.

I also met a handsome, dark-haired stranger that morning.

I haven't been keeping up with things for a while. I stay up quite late because I'm writing a book and starting a business. Since I've resolved to be more social, I'm also hearing from many friends, and everyone has compelling things to share. I fall into heart-to-heart conversations with other women who notice that I've transformed from wallflower to sunflower and, with their dreams piqued, ask about my story.

So, sometimes I wake up later than I used to, and when that happens, I quickly throw on any old thing (OK, it's not any old thing. Today, I've thrown on stockings, a cream wool dress, and black high heels). After that, though... I'm flying to work. Truly. And maybe I'm flying because we, witches, fly. Ha, ha.

I usually enter the cafe, greet employees and other guests with a sincere "Good morning" and order my favorite salad. I pay, smile, and leave. Usually.

I don't know why, but something stops me in my tracks. I look to the left and see a handsome, dark-haired man sitting and drinking coffee. He smiles at me, and sends me a kiss. In return, I tell him:

"I will send you one right back."

We both smile, and then I nearly dance out the door.

After a few metres, I stopped and asked myself: Should I go back? I don't, but I wonder what would have happened if I had.

I often walk through my favorite park on my way back from the office. Today, brilliant autumn colours draw me here. I lay down in one of the hammocks hung between the trees. It is beautiful and warm.

"Whatever" I think. "I'll decompress a little."

Lying on my back, I took a deep breath, as if I wanted to get to the real scent of autumn. I closed my eyes. The delicate swaying of the hammock and the sound of the trees put me into a light trance. I didn't think about anything, I just admired the blue sky and gave in to the music of rustling leaves in the wind.

Just me, myself, and I.

It got so blissful that I started to miss my man. I took the phone out of my pocket and recorded a short video. I surprised myself with how beautiful I looked. A face emanating the flush of love, sun kissed cheeks. I was a Cherub who has just descended from paradise called Love. My eyes sparkled in the light, and my lips looked full and beautiful. I could have fallen in love with myself. “It’s probably about time that you did” I told myself. Ha, ha.

A few days before my trip to Italy, Fulvio sent me a photo. In a sea of about twenty athletic, striking men captured on a tennis court, my gaze unfailingly found him. He wasn't the most conspicuous among them, a brunette without the sculpted physique of Adonis, but there was his smile, a particular expression that rendered everyone else insignificant. Every shred of doubt evaporated when my eyes fell on his image. He was the one, unequivocally and irresistibly.

I texted:

“You’re the only one for me, darling. I’m sure of it.”

The long-awaited day finally arrived. Trip to Italy? No, no - not yet. Today was a great day, because boy-wonder is celebrating a birthday.

I had been planning a special birthday present for weeks. It would definitely be a movie. The main role played by stockings and garters, which I like so much which drive him crazy.

How did I do it?

I put on lace underwear, stockings with a garter belt, and of course, high heels.

I lay down on the bed... and what next?

No, not so fast.

I took a birthday greeting card from the drawer, which I had already written, and put it on my lace-wrapped thighs. I took a few photos. I recorded a short video.

"No, something's not right" I thought. "Something is missing ... I know, I need music."

I opened my laptop and I found a piano version of "Happy Birthday" online. This was it!

I looked at my watch. Unfortunately, it was already after midnight, and I had hoped to premiere my film at midnight.

I started playing the song video. The pianist sat down and touched the keys. First vigorously, then with care and sensitivity. The instrument reacted immediately, making sweet sounds. This brilliant couple created something inspiring, touching, and soothing - music.

I dedicated the first frame of the video to a beautiful, silvery-blue birthday card with an engraved "Happy Birthday." Then the camera showed my dainty feet in satin high heels and one charming bow on my stockings. The shot moved up and after a while my slim and sculpted calves dressed in elegant black stockings topped with miniature bows appeared on the screen. A moment later, the eye of the camera reaches my thighs, beautifully wrapped with lace. Now lace underwear came into view, above which you can see a delicate navel and, above it, the garter belt.

The pianist ends the performance, and my recording also ends.

At 7:00 am, I listen to a loud:

"Wooooooow!" And then, "Thank you, thank you, thank you. Thank you very much."

* * *

On Thursday morning, I'm awoken by a flock of butterflies in my stomach. There are so many of them that the strength of their delicate wings almost lifts my body. I lie in my comfortable bed, wrapped in beautiful bedding. I gently touch my belly and cleavage.

Yes, I feel it. I am an awakened woman who knows what she wants.

I'm not ashamed to think about it or to talk about it anymore. I don't want to have sex with a man anymore. I want to make love with him.

Maybe you will ask what the difference is?

Once upon a time, I couldn't have answered, because I used these phrases interchangeably, but since Italy invited me to its bedroom, I see and feel the difference.

I want my closeness with a man to be full of passion and mindfulness. I don't want a race to an orgasm. I want to feel everything.

For me, to make love to a man means to unite with him in the act of elation. To feel his body like you feel your own. Sink into each other and melt into caresses. It's to really see each other and open yourself to all of the sensations. It is complete trust and mutual devotion. It is looking deeply into your lover's eyes and seeing yourself reflected back, bathed in love. To feel delicate brushes of bodies, give in to the rhythm of breath and react to the heat and chills of ecstasy. And the most wonderful thing is that you can feel all these experiences, only by laying body to body with your love.

I don't want to hurry. I want attention.

I want to dance like lovers who do not plan and think during the rapprochement.

I want to dance the dance of lovers who give in fully to their feelings.

I write:

"Dearest. I miss you. The waiting is becoming unbearable. There are only two days to our meeting, but these two days feel like eternity. I want you to hug me, look into my eyes, and give me that *Hey, my sweet.*"

I hope that my charming Sicilian is only having this effect on me. Otherwise, I'm in trouble.

The lesson I learned is: I wasn't born to be a saint!

The lesson you learned is:

....

....

....

....

....

....

....

....

....

....

....

....

....

....

....

....

....

....

....

....

....

....

....

....

....

....

....

....

Back in Paradise

I'm sick. Covid is prowling out in the world, and my joints hurt. I haven't been feeling the best since Tuesday. My head had hurt all day. I was sure that it was only a short-term migraine, but on Wednesday I developed aches between my shoulder blades. That can only mean one thing - the flu.

This is just what I needed.

I have been waiting two months for a meeting with my love, and now some stupid flu will thwart my plans? Never. I will not give up!

I take work home and I start heavy treatment. High doses of vitamin C, aspirin, and ginger. I hope that'll be enough. I'm relieved that I do not have a fever, because otherwise, it'd be game over for getting on a plane.

Since the change in my well-being, I feel somehow muted. I don't know why. I feel strangely distant from everything. My movements are slightly slowed down, my fervent thoughts have died down.

Interesting.

On Thursday, in my therapy session with Julia, I learn something: frightening yourself, building bleak scenarios and catastrophizing are symptoms of a lack of trust in life. There's something to this.

How do we trust life? How can we let go of control? How can we catch a wave and ride it where it might take us? How can we wake up every morning with curiosity about what the day will bring us, not with fear of what might happen? It is not easy, especially when you grew up in a super controlling household. I don't blame my parents these days though, I know they did the best they could.

I think of the old saying, "you can't get blood from a stone." I know my parents couldn't give me more than what they had. I have long been reconciled with them and I love them more than life itself, but I still have a hard time trusting because of them. Especially when I care about something and I'm afraid I will lose it.

Wistfulness comes over me.

"Maybe I will watch a movie?" I think.

My English teacher suggested that I watch movies to practice pronunciation and to build my vocabulary. I look for a movie he recommended to me, but can't find it. So I search for just "a movie in English with Polish subtitles" and the only option I'm served up is: "The Visitation" directed by David A .R. White. I watch and... I stop believing in coincidence. The plot talks about rebuilding trust in our Creator. Not everything in the movie appeals to me, but a few themes affect me so much that as the end credits roll, I sit on my sofa with tears flowing down my cheeks, with love in my heart and a cry on my lips:

"Universe, lead me! I want to be the best person I can be. I trust love, love will always win."

Suddenly, as if by magic, my beloved calls me. He wants to know what I'm doing, how I'm feeling, and he asks me if I'm ready for our visit. He's missing me and is waiting for me impatiently.

* * *

At last!!! Today is the big day! My dreams are coming true! After two months of waiting - I'm returning to my Eden. Waiting for this was difficult and I hope that instead of overthinking, I'll be able to enjoy the present moment.

In a few hours I will see Fulvio, I will be able to hug him and feel the closeness that I've missed.

In the morning a short telephone conversation and an exchange of kisses. We reassure each other that we want this meeting and we can't wait for it.

At 12:00 pm, I send a photo from the airport and in return I receive a charming:

"Yeah!!!!!"

I get on the plane with my new friends, who didn't believe in love after 40 - Magda and Beata. I take my seat and send him a photo showing the aircraft wing against the background of the blue sky covered with delicate, fluffy clouds. It's unbelievable how different things look when you're seeing the world from a bird's eye view. Up here, you can truly embrace the majesty of mountain ranges, rise above the cloud ceiling and feel not like the ruler, but like a tiny piece of the world.

A message on WhatsApp.

"Yes!! Have a safe flight, honey."

I realize that in just two hours my dreams will come true. Exactly two months ago, I was standing at the Bologna airport, cuddled into Fulvio's arms as he kissed me tenderly on the lips, forehead and eyes.

That was the first time I told him that I liked him very much. Yes, I remember every second of that meeting.

I have never met a man whose gaze was so pure and deep. I don't like comparisons, so I'll just say that I have never met another man who gave such juicy kisses, uplifted me, and was as brilliant and warm.

It's impossible to describe precisely, but if you saw me, you'd understand.

After warm farewell hugs with my travel companions, who inspired in me a belief in miracles and a new life, I send a short:

"I'm here."

I'm sure that Marta, Beata, and I will remember our conversation for the rest of our lives. I am grateful that I could inspire these two women and give them hope. In turn, their fascination and joy gave me strength and confirmed my belief that the path I am on is the right one and that as soon as I spread my wings a bit more, I will fly.

I'm waiting for my beloved. He texts that he will be there in a moment. He's here!

He gets out of the car and waves cheerfully at me. It's him! The same sparkling, gorgeous eyes, the same radiant smile.

I'm sure I'm his! When we embrace each other, I feel it so clearly. This is something real. I come close, kiss him on the lips, and snuggle into his arms as deeply as I can to feel enveloped in a blanket of warmth and love. He's here! My beloved! A familiar scent and his body close to me. With my eyes closed, I would have found his hands among a hundred others touching my body and I would have recognized his voice among a million other voices floating in the wind. This feels right. I'm happy.

My gentleman opens the car door for me, I get in, and we drive. Another dozen kisses connect us. The kisses are necessary to see if everything still works and to remind our bodies of each other. There is blissful peace. Looking slightly concerned, Fulvio asks:

"Why are you so quiet?"

"I'm just happy" I answer.

I'm a high-energy person, and sometimes I get fired up. I can shout for joy and give in to complete excitement. Then I talk like crazy and gesticulate wildly. My daughter has shushed me more than once, saying: "Mom, you're acting like a teenager." I always answer the same way: "Darling, everyone has to live their youth someday. I didn't get a chance to do this as a teenager, so let me do it now. I've worked hard for it."

However, there are situations when I celebrate happiness in silence. Then, I feel blissful peace and a sense of fulfillment. It's a state like the one I found myself in after opening the parachute during my first jump.

"I'm quiet when I'm happiest" I explain to Fulvio. With an understanding smile and a hug, we go home to a house near Bologna, in a wonderful, quiet (there's that quiet again) area. Where the greenery is strikingly similar to the one in the park near my house. Where songbirds bustle among the cedar branches all day long, looking for snacks. Where dogs lounge lazily on freshly mown grass, and the only effort they can muster is to twitch their ears in search of any disturbing sound that could signal the end of their nap.

A familiar, squeaky gate, a familiar mailbox, greeting neighbours, a door inviting you to enter and… Home, sweet home. A place dear to me, filled with the same scent of Italian perfume I remembered. This mixture of the sweetness of hard candy, the sourness and depth of lime... this space envelops you. I calmly enter the bedroom, open my suitcase and…

"What are you doing?" Fulvio asks.

"I have something for you, honey" I reply, taking out two frames with my photos and a blue and silver birthday card. "I brought you a birthday present."

"Thank you very much" I hear and receive a sweet kiss.

"Any interest in making love to me?" He asks shyly.

"Oh, definitely" I reply and we're already in a passionate embrace. At that moment, I dream of nothing more than to feel his naked body next to me, above me and inside me.

Instead of wasting time on taking our clothes off layer by layer, we immediately shake off everything. We jump into bed like a couple of teenagers waiting anxiously for their first time. He leans over me and kisses my lips, neck and cleavage tenderly. I raise my legs so that my feet touch the mattress. In a gesture of invitation, I open my thighs, and he gently fills me and hugs me tightly. We want to be as close to each other as possible. Fulvio sinks into me even more tenderly, and I feel true pleasure as I place my calves on his shoulders. Just like two months ago, I ask "Dear moment, please last forever."

"I would like to collect my birthday present" he says.

"Please. I'm all yours" I whisper.

He flips me from the back to the front, spreads my thighs and penetrates me passionately. Then he puts his hands under my stomach, lifts me up and buries himself in me again, causing me to experience ecstasy.

After a while, sitting on him, wrapping my naked thighs around him and looking into his eyes, I once again have the opportunity to feel excitement mixed with intoxication.

Losing my gaze in his chocolate eyes is like taking an express ride to paradise. I grab his hands and lift them high above his head. He's on his back, underneath me, I'm above him. Who is the driver and who is the passenger? How will this romantic journey end? We don't care!

I didn't make up Fulvio. Now I know it. He is just like I remembered him. We caress each other passionately, surrendering to our emotions. Hungry for kisses and touches, I want more and more.

In the afternoon, a short tour of Bologna. Fulvio's friend takes us to Santuario Madonna di San Luca. The monumental sanctuary where the painting of the Madonna is kept is place of pilgrimage. The faithful from all over Italy visit this place, and those brave souls who want to reach the basilica on foot must traverse the longest portico in the world (3,796 meters).

I love old, colossal architecture. It always gives me a kind of déjà vu.

My mind takes me back to many years ago, when among the residents bustling in a hurry of their daily affairs I would see dust-covered children playing with abandon. There is nothing more beautiful than the freedom of childhood.

After the walk, dinner. "Where?" You ask.

Naturally, we go to a pizzeria. I love Italian food, especially in Italy. Original products, fresh vegetables and fruit, and pure olive oil bring both lightness and depth of flavour to Italian dishes. Two pizzas shine beautifully on our plates, like two full moons, covered with a blanket of fresh mozzarella. On it, as if scattered timidly, slightly salty, aromatic, big brown olives. Next to them, juicy and crisp leaves of fresh basil and pieces of sundried tomatoes create harmony. As a tradition now, we share each other's pizzas. And we talk. I feel protected.

Late in the evening we return to the bedroom to once again indulge in the pleasure of our love then, cuddling together, fall asleep.

When I left for Bologna, I promised myself that I would tell Fulvio what I felt. I had some kind of a plan after all. Ha, ha.

I wanted to start a conversation on Sunday evening, but I gave up.

"Why?" You ask.

Sunday was too wonderful. At 7:00 am I was woken up by my birthday present. Tender caresses. First, gentle strokes on my neck, sending a wave of shivers starting at the base of my breasts, rising to my nipples, and breaking lightly over my belly.

"Let's go back to the neck" I requested.

While his lips tasted me tenderly, his hand went on a wondrous journey towards my womb, ending where I liked it best - inside me. Once again I felt a wave of pleasure rising gently from my stomach, and after a while it covered my whole body; starting from the top of my head and ending at my feet. I compare this feeling to levitation, in which instead of your body you only feel a tingling lifting you above the bed.

My master's hand moves slowly towards my hips and thighs and ends its journey, stroking my calves and feet.

I hear a sensual:

"Happy birthday, dear. This is your day. Do with me what you like."

A knowing smile, a deep look into our eyes and we don't need anything else to be happy!

Let's sail!

We enjoy a typical Italian breakfast: cake and coffee. It's cake and water with lemon for me, because I don't drink coffee, although in moments like these, I think about learning to like it because some things require coffee - like eating an Italian cornetto for example.

We set out for a motorcycle ride.

The weather is not the best, but what wouldn't any of us do to feel the wind in our hair and the kick of adrenaline?

I had no idea that at the age of fifty-four I would become a motorcycling enthusiast. OK, I like driving fast and I have a "led foot" as they say, but a motorbike is a completely different experience. You sit comfortably in a car. A safe cabin surrounds you, your favorite music plays on the radio. You're driving fast, but it's still like you're licking candy through a foil wrapper.

A motorbike is like a gust of wind. It is feeling speed with every part of your body. A bike does not forgive poor cooperation. He is like a demanding but generous lover who requires attention, but in return gives real satisfaction. I sit comfortably in the passenger position, with my feet on the footrests. I'm dressed in my partner's oversized but warm jacket, helmet and men's gloves, I wrap my thighs around his hips (ooh, ooh) and press my breasts against his back. I love riding with Fulvio. He is the best driver I have ever had the opportunity to travel with. We reach a speed of one hundred and seventy kilometers per hour and his BMW is floats down the road.

A TRIO OF LOVERS - THE MOTORBIKE, FULVIO AND ME.

Here we go!

We want to eat lunch in a countryside restaurant, but to get there we have to get to crowded Bologna. We choose to travel to the city center on the Marconi Express high-speed train. We have two options to reach the Old Town. The first one is a long walk, the second one is a crazy scooter trip. OK, but let's not get ahead of the story.

We had planned to rent two scooters, but unfortunately - or maybe fortunately - the rental system did not work, and we were left to travel in tandem on a single-person scooter. Ha ha! In the driver position stands Fulvio, and behind him, with her arms around his waist, Iwona. One foot on the scooter platform and the other on the fender. Ha, ha.

We're off.

The old town welcomed us with sunny weather and an incredibly large crowds of tourists. I will not forget this ride for the rest of my life.

First time on a scooter.

First time on a single-person scooter as a duo.

Was it like returning to the carefree days of childhood? Maybe, although I don't remember my childhood as carefree. That was not a happy time for me, but fortunately my inner child and I know how to feel carefree now.

We drive at twenty-five kilometers an hour through the streets of ancient Bologna, trying to avoid tourists with a warning "Pi, piii!" on the lips. One-way streets, no turn signal lights, whatever...

In love and happy.

TWO KIDS - A ONE PERSON SCOOTER - BROKEN BELL

Fulvio and I were two energies that harmonized perfectly with each other. Yes, Julia, you were right - with him there will always be joy and fun.

Time to head back to his house near Bologna.

We are waiting at the train station. A large number of passengers gathers around, including a tearful brown-haired woman with hazel eyes. She has a backpack and a carry-on bag with her. I guess that her final destination will be the airport. I glance at her. I would like to ask her if she's OK and why she is crying, but I don't speak Italian well enough. She boards the same Marconi Express train carriage as us. It's very crowded. Fortunately for us, this journey is only one stop. We get off, and the brown-haired woman does too. We go down the stairs towards his parked car and hear her exclaim:

"Oh no! Where am I? Where is airport?"

Fulvio approaches her, explaining that she got off one stop too early.

"Oh no!" she sobs. "My plane boards in 20 minutes."

"That's a bit of a tough assignment, but get in. We will take you to the airport" I hear a calming pronouncement from Fulvio.

We get her there and she is very grateful. We stand in front of the departures hall. He gets out of the car in a hurry, thanks us with a sunny smile and runs...

After a moment of silence I tell Fulvio:

"What you did was really kind. Thank you."

In the evening, dinner at home. I love watching a man embrace cooking. There's an enchantment to how precisely he chops the ingredients, how thoroughly he mixes them and seasones them to taste. Then he calls me and asks:

"Give it a taste, my love. Is it missing anything?"

"It's perfect" I respond. "This will be the finest cooking I'll have here."

I look as he carefully sets the table for us and fills our glasses with red wine.

"Please, sit down" he extends a polite invite.

That evening we eat spaghetti with garlic and truffles. It's the first time I try this combination of flavours. After our lovely dinner, we lie cuddled on the sofa, watching a rugby match (Fulvio's favorite team is playing). And again I beseech the universe: "Dear moment, please last forever."

I am awestruck by how little we actually need to be happy, to achieve a sense of fulfillment, to feel accepted and loved. It's wonderful that people can give to each other what they cannot find in themselves…

I quietly slipped out of Fulvio's arms and went to the bathroom. I had promised that I would bring the stockings, garter belt and high heels, which my lover adores.

When I came out in my sexy ensemble, he was already waiting in the bedroom. I walked confidently, on my slim, stocking-covered legs. I bowed my head and kissed his lips. I sat with my lace-wrapped bottom on his naked hips.

Two small, round breasts peeked out from under the tightly fitting lace corset.

"Your tits make me happy." I heard him say and then an inferno of desire roared up inside of me.

* * *

Unfortunately, time waits for no one and my stay in paradise has come to an end. Our last morning together arrived. A quick coffee, a kiss and a hug.

"The weather is gloomy today, just like my heart" said Fulvio .

I kissed him tenderly.

In the car on our way to the airport I had the last chance to say how I felt.

Before I started, he took my hand, plaited my fingers tightly with his and pulled me towards him. I took a deep breath, sighed and started to speak.

"Do you remember our last farewell at the Bologna airport?"

"Yes, I remember" he replied.

"And do you remember what I told you then? I said I like you very much…"

I took a short pause. "Things have changed." I added.

I felt him withdraw slightly with a chill. He smiled crookedly and, as if encouraging himself with laughter, asked:

"Why? Do you have someone else in Poland?"

"Things have changed because I've fallen in love with you" I said.

Fulvio's reaction was the most wonderful gift I could have expected from this man who didn't like to write or talk a lot. He held on to my hand more tightly, and embraced me. He breathed a sigh of relief. His face transformed from a tense, forced smile to gentle happiness. It gave me the curouage to keep talking.

"I've fallen in love with you and I would like to be your girlfriend" I said.

"But you're already my girlfriend" he replied.

"It makes me so happy to hear you say that" I added with elation in my voice.

"Since we're deciding to be a couple we should get to know each other better" I continued. "I would like to give our relationship a chance. I know that your work schedule won't allow you to travel to me, but I'm happy to come here. I can visit you even every two or three weeks. For example, next week I have Thursday off, so I could come…"

I didn't finish because Fulvio, with his characteristic quiet firmness, interrupted me and said:

"That's impossible, dear. In November and December I have a ton of work."

His words floored me. I froze in silence.

Eventually I uttered "OK", not wanting to continue this topic, lest, God forbid, I hear something even more unpleasant.

It wouldn't have taken much for me to burst into tears and yell: "*If you don't want my visit, fine, see if I care. Goodbye!*" I didn't do it because after this visit my goose was cooked. I was already head over heels in love. I preferred to live in a reality where I would be able to change his mind later.

"OK. I'll send you some possible flights later" I said quietly.

"OK."

We arrived at the airport. He got out of the car, opened the door, hugged me and kissed me.

In between the kisses, I whispered:

"Ti amo, ti amo."

“Me too, honey” he replied. He looked into my eyes. “Please don't cry” he whispered sweetly. “Goodbye.”

That word stung me and made me uneasy.

“Please don’t say goodbye” I asked. “Tell me - see you later”

“See you” he obliged.

One last kiss goodbye and was time to leave paradise.

The lesson I learned is: Don’t be afraid to say what you feel.

The lesson you learned is:

....

....

....

....

....

....

....

....

....

....

....

....

....

....

....

....

....

....

....

....

....

....

....

....

....

....

....

....

Rollercoaster In Poland

"I've arrived in Warsaw"

"Thank you for letting me know, my sweet. Is everything OK?"

"Yes."

...that's what I wrote, but everything was far from OK.

* * *

When he had dropped me off at the Bologna airport it was nearly empty.

"Why did he bring me here so early" I started wondering. "It's 7:00 am. We had planned that he'd drop me off at the airport at 8:00 am. Now I'm stuck here with absolutely nothing to do for two and a half hours.. We could have still been snuggled together" I thought, irritated. I felt like he had robbed me of that hour. An hour that was priceless to me.

On the plane I looked through our photos, hunting for a picture I could post online. This wasn't spur off the moment idea. I had thought about it while planning my trip. I wanted to take a nice photo and post it on Facebook, but first I would ask Fulvio's permission. Now that I thought about it, I was a bit surprised at myself. Why would I ask him for permission? It was my Facebook profile and he's divorced, what could be the issue?

I texted:

"My love, could I post a photo of us to my FB?"

"Please don't. I'm still battling my wife's lawyers."

I felt as if someone had unplugged my power cord. I didn't even have the strength to get angry. My intuition must have been picking up something, that's why I got the hunch to ask first.

"I'm sorry, my sweet."

I slept the rest of the flight. It was easier that way, but after leaving the airport I couldn't keep it together anymore. I started crying. First quietly, then fully sobbing and wailing. Without shame and without embarrassment. I wasn't going to hide. My whole being wept: heart, soul and body.

On an intercity train, I could tell that the other passengers were looking at me furtively.

I know, I know. A crying woman is going to draw attention. Just like that beautiful woman I had seen on the Marconi Express. We had all looked at her, but no one had the guts to ask her what happened. I learned a life lesson then, I'll never just ignore a crying person again.

For a while I was sitting next to a group of young men who were having an energetic conversation. One of them was watching me closely. After a while he sat down in front of me and asked:

"Excuse me, ma'am, did something happen?"

"No no, it's just falling in love."

"Oh. Is that good or bad?"

"I don't know. It's hard to say at the moment" I sobbed.

After a moment's pause, he handed me a handkerchief, looked into my eyes with his dark eyes and added:

"You look stunning when you cry."

This broke me. I ugly-cried the entire train ride, on the tram and even as I walked through my beloved park. Upon returning to my apartment, a profound sense of emptiness and loneliness overwhelmed me.

I picked up my phone and wrote:

"Honey, I can't lie. Everything is not OK. I'm like that woman from the Marconi Express, only even more tearful."

"You're an exceptional woman."

Unimpressed with Fulvio's response, I wrote:

"My love, as promised, I've checked the flights from Warsaw to Bologna. In November I can fly in on a Friday or a Saturday and return on a Sunday or a Monday. What do you say to another weekend, just the two of us? I think you deserve a bit of relaxation and I'd like to care of you. Spending quality time with the man I love and who loves me is important, necessary and non-negotiable for me. I await your answer."

I sent it, and then immediately flooded my mind with catastrophic scenarios. I quickly recalled myself together and instead of imagining what could happen, how and when; I started dancing.

I remembered the words a wonderful coach who saved me after my break up with my ex - and Julia's tips - that love is strong and will always defend itself. Fleeting infatuations are not real love, if they fade so be it. I calmed down.

I waited calmly, because love cannot be lost. When one runs out, you get double.

* * *

I woke up angry. Yes, angry. Fulvio was active on WhatsApp at 12:47 am, read my message and didn't reply. Prickly as a porcupine and spoiling for a fight, I thought:

"Please, don't do me any favors. Whatever. I wonder what he was doing from 8:00 pm to nearly one in the morning?" I asked myself, full of anger and hurt. He wasn't in our chat. There could only be one answer: he was meeting another woman.

I was torn by conflicting emotions - from love to anger. "Oh, this Fulvio, he's a real Casanova" I thought and smiled. "I'm not writing to him until he reaches out first."

At 8:00 am I received a "letter."

> "Buon giorno! Dearest, as I told you, November is super tought for me. I have a lot going on at work. I'm very busy. Maybe it would be better to plan our reunion in December? I was really happy when you were here…"

I sent him a recorded, short but joyful "Good morning!"

Truthfully, I was even more ticked off than before. I felt rejected. As soon as I stopped feeling the childish hurt of not getting exactly what I wanted, I sent him a short "ti amo" and in return I received a big red heart. I was happy. No, I wasn't waiting for a "ti amo" back. I didn't send it to fish a declaration of love from him. Why? Because I was learning to do what I feel is right, regardless of the consequences and without preconceived expectations. This was a huge challenge for me.

My goal is to achieve such equilibrium in life that I will be able to live:

- without fear of judgment,
- without fear of rejection,
- without fear of losing self-respect,
- without fear of ridicule,
- without fear of losing dignity,
- without fear of losing love...

… able to do and say what I feel.

My therapy practice has shown me that you can't lose your dignity by saying that you love someone and want to be with them. The truth cannot rob us of our dignity.

Lies and manipulation rob us of our dignity.

If someone scoffs at your "I'd like to be with you" it's not your problem; it's theirs. They have shown you that they have a problem accepting the truth of others.

Who would laugh at a person opening their heart and revealing their most vulnerable spots? Only someone afraid of being ridiculed themselves.

Let's not be afraid to do what we feel. Let's not allow ourselves to be robbed of the courage to be ourselves here and now. Let's talk openly about our needs and feelings.

What can those who would hurt us really do to us? What can a person, whose fear of feeling is so great that he must disguise it with laughter, mockery, and irony, accomplish?

Do what you feel, don't postpone feeling.

Halfway through the day, I wrote flirtatiously:

"What is my handsome man up to?"

...and I found out that he was in a meeting.

In the afternoon I sent him flight options for December and...

Well, my old self would have waited with a stopwatch in her hand for an answer. Every minute of waiting would be agony. Today I stoped to think(!): "Give him time to decide. Let him think about the best date for your arrival. Maybe he needs to consult his work or family. Give him time, and don't smother him, forcing a quick answer. People are different. Not everyone is like you and loves to act spontaneously, to drop everything at a moment's notice."

Maybe he also needs time to think through everything that's happened between us?

Maybe the fact that we confessed our love to each other is like jumping into the deep end for him too?

Maybe he didn't fully realize he was dealing with a woman who knew what she wanted from life but was sensitive and delicate deep down?

Maybe this situation is a tough nut for him to crack? Maybe he had expected that things wouldn't change for him?

After this reflection, I decided to give him time. So instead of texting him a question like: "Were you planning on answering?" or "How much time do you need to respond to me?" I wrote:

"My love, I am lying alone in my huge bed and I'm thinking about those wonderful moments when I was so close to and happy with you. When I felt your body next to mine all night long, when I reacted to your every move and you did to mine. When we were a tangle of arms wrapped around

> each other. When I did everything to keep my body close to yours. When even my feet clung to your feet, when my thighs nestled against your manly thighs, when your hips wrapped around mine like a protective armor. When you placed your hands on my waist like a guard signaling that I was yours."

* * *

Great plans and aspirations are great, but the heart wants what it wants.

I sit and sob. Fulvio still has not responded to my proposal to visit in December. If this had happened to me with any previous guy, I would have put an end to the mess (as my dad used to say) a long time ago. I'd send a message like: "Get lost, good luck" and start a new life.

It's different with Fulvio. I don't love his behaviour, yet I feel there is something there. I don't know if it's instinct, a fatal attraction, or maybe the universe's plan?

Here I am, dancing with joy, lighthearted, fired up to get things done, delighted with my new life, and then a lack of a message from my man can topple my intricately built world. I pine, and I wait. I miss him so much. I would like to hug him again, hear his wonderful voice, and feel the bliss and peace I had felt while lying on the couch with him and watching the rugby match.

The hardest thing to deal with is the fear. Fear of losing the love surging through me.

The last time when I prioritized love was a very long time ago. Then for a decade, I did everything I could to prevent love from even sprouting in my heart, let alone growing there. But everything was different now? Yes, because I got hit by Cupid's arrow, without having any real say about it. The long-resisted feeling washed over me like a tsunami, giving me neither the opportunity to reason, nor time to calculate potential risks and rewards.

When I'm in love, I'm like a powder pink jewelry box with miniature drawers and a small mirror, on public display. Open to everyone. Everyone can look.

Now that I have fallen in love with being in love - a state that's lifting me higher than everything I have previously felt - I feel more faith in people, have a higher regard for men, and am learning humility and patience.

"This relationship did not arrive in your life to give you peace and solace, but to wake you up. There is no greater teacher than such a relationship" I heard from my therapist and friend Bartek.

So I sit and cry. I cry for myself, I cry with longing, I cry with fear, I cry with loneliness... I cry.

I think about him, me, and the beautiful moments we spent in Bologna. I feel the gust of wind in my sunny hair as I stood right behind him on the scooter, utterly free from worries and so happy.

I close my eyes, let out a sigh, and tears begin to flow down my cheeks like liquid pearls.

With each inhale I feel enormous gratitude for what I am experiencing.

Each exhale is like a new declaration of my love.

"Go ahead and cry, my love" my friend Gosia once said to me. "I'm so sorry you're hurting. I am so sad that you are crying. Still, I am glad you are having this experience because purification and transformation will come with it.

And although it's hard for me to imagine the transformation that Gosia is talking about, I let my feelings guide me because I don't want to live any other way. I want to be honest with myself and the world. No pretences, no masks. I want to heal from everything that burdens me and prevents me from living in truth, love, and respect for others.

I want to feel what true love means - unselfish, devoted and respecting the other person's needs.

* * *

All of the clothes that I brought from Bologna smell like his house.

Another day with no answer from Fulvio regarding our meeting in December. But the man is putting forth an effort overall. Every day he greets me with a "good morning" and yesterday he said goodbye with a sweet "Good night, my treasure". It's incredible how these words lift my spirit.

I remind myself to listen to what people say, not what they haven't said. Read what people write, not what they haven't written. He has never written that he doesn't want to see me, that I should get lost. He just wrote that November was a very hard month for him at home and work, so maybe it would be better to plan our meeting for December. OK.

Another lonely evening, and I ponder whether to send him a flirtatious "buonanotte" or to get offended that he didn't answer my "ti amo."

How long will I be tossed in the tempest of these emotional extremes, leading me from love to anger?

Will I ever achieve a balance that will allow me to accept human choices with humility and peace?

How long will I treat not replying to my message, as a slight towards me?

How long will the words of my grandmothers, aunts and my mother, who, like an oracle, declared: "never let them see that you care" ring in my head?

When will I accept that everyone has the right to write what they want, when they want, and relax about it?

Today, a little wiser, I know that the only thing I can do is accept it or move on.

"My freedom ends where yours begins." Those were some of the first words Fulvio said to me. They didn't mean much to me the first time I heard them. An obvious truism. Today, I find them more and more meaningful, and I feel them more and more deeply.

The lesson I learned is: My freedom ends where yours begins.

The lesson you learned is:

My Tribe

On Saturday - another weekend with Italy further in my rear view mirror - my weekly 5Rhythms dynamic movement practice class saved me. 5Rhythms is a movement meditation practice created by Gabrielle Roth in the late 1970s that draws from indigenous and world traditions. It's incredible how quickly this practice has become a natural part of my life and how much I get out of it. During one of these workshops, I learned how our needs change over time and how important it is to listen to them.

Earlier I had joined a tantric meditation women's circle run by my friend Marta.

Wonderful meetings full of feminine energy, peace, reflection, and self-acceptance. I was particularly moved by exercises that involved looking straight into the eyes of other women. It's incredible how much fear, suffering, and uncertainty you can see in them, intertwined with love and strength. It was an unforgettable feeling.

It was time for changes. I didn't plan them. They just happened.

My friend Aldonka, unable to watch me suffering madly in love with Fulvio, invited me to a workshop and I went.

My friend Marta called me many times with an invitation to her women's circle meetings, and I'd answer:

"Dear, thank you for the invite. If it's not an inconvenience for you to keep sharing the workshop info with me, please continue to do so, because I will return to workshops one day, but not now. Right now, I feel myself pulled in a different direction. I need to dance with my tribe."

I want to feel the five rhythms that bring me to life: *Flowing, Staccato, Chaos, Lyric* and *Stillness*. I want to find contact with the earth and return to my roots in the rhythm of the feminine *Flowing*. I love to immerse myself in *Staccato* and feel the masculine fire that releases courage in me. I want to learn to let go of control and lose everything unnecessary in the rhythm of *Chaos*. I want to know my authentic movement, feel lightness and freedom in *Lyric* energy. I dream of dancing with my soul, connecting with my inner silence, and being reconciled with everything in *Stillness*.

When I entered the 5Rhythms dance studio and heard the first beats of music, I burst into tears. Tears fell down my face like diamonds. They were tears of longing for my Italian boyfriend, hurt that he wasn't giving me what I needed, and resignation. I cried out my loneliness while massaging my feet and hands.

"I love you so much" I said to myself. "I'm so sorry that you're hurting. All I can do is be there for you and comfort you like a sister." Nothing is more beautiful than words of tenderness and love spoken to ourselves.

My tribe was slowly joining the class. New participants came in one after another.

Those I knew greeted me with friendly glances. I couldn't wait for the warm-up rhythms. At the beginning of the class, our instructor asks us to set our intention. This mobilized my gray cells, and the first thought that came to my mind was: "*I trust you, life. Guide me.*" After class, I was struck by a realization that I had come here with a different need - a vast longing for a man, for his touch and presence. And what did I get?

In the first rhythms of Staccato, I found myself side by side with Tomasz. He placed his head on my belly and we swam. It was a rhythmic dance of two searching spirits. We gave each other the attention and touch we both needed. After a while, the dance floor connected me with another man. We focused on the dance.

We reacted to each other's every gesture, breath, and movement. We sailed in trust, closeness, and respect. As my partner lifted me off the dance floor and I wrapped my thighs around his hips, he sighed and hugged me tightly. At times, we experienced an ecstasy comparable to that experienced by lovers, with one difference. When you practice the 5Rhythms dance, you direct your sexual energy from your body to your heart and soul.

For the part of the practice where I could dip into madness and release my anger, I partnered with a charming brunette, Vadim. We were both bursting with vigor. With each vocalization, with each grimace, we released anger, discord, and the norms that limit us. Our bodies cowered in fear and showed us animal ferocity. How spontaneous can you be? Can you disconnect your mind and follow the music? All it takes is a quick reset, and you're good to go. In one moment, such intense energy was created between my and my partner's hands that we felt a vibrating warmth. We had fun, moving our hands apart and closer. I experimented, trying to direct this wave. Several times during that evening, energy connected me with wonderful partners.

When we sat in a circle at the end of the class, I was overcome with enormous gratitude.

I said:

"My name is Iwona. I wanted to thank you, instructor, for today's class. Thank you all of you who danced here today, but especially I wanted to thank all of my male partners who gave me their attention and touch. I needed male energy and the closeness of a male body today. We need you like water to flowers, without you life would have no meaning. Thank you."

An appreciative murmur spread across the room and I felt grateful. I was grateful to my friend for inviting me to this meditation practice. This was exactly what I needed at this stage of my life, and I each time I participated in a class I felt it with more certainty.

Dancing liberates me. I've always liked dancing. I once said that water is my element. I take to water, well, like a fish to water. I'm not afraid of water, on the contrary, the agitated it is, the more fun and satisfaction I feel when swimming. I love being fully immersed in water's flow, recording all of the sounds that reach my ears, all of the sights. It's as if I were on the other side of the mirror and was observing my body with fascination.

However, since I discovered 5Rhythms dance meditation, I realized that water is an element that I became friends with because I practiced swimming for hours. Dance is an element that has always been in me. I'm naturally attuned to music and movement.

We gather at the doors of Club Milonga. I joyfully greet Vadim, that sensitive brunette who was such a wonderful partner to me during the last class, joined me in dancing like a pair of kids - going crazy and letting out alternating anger and joy.

He greets me in the best way. This almost two-meter tall man grabs me with his strong arms, lifts me, hugs me tightly and says:

"Iwonka, I missed you so much and I was afraid you wouldn't come today."

"I missed you too" I respond honestly. "I'm so glad you're here."

We spent a few minutes hugging as if the rest of the world didn't exists. After a while, Tom joined the group. Last Saturday, he and I were a pair of lovers craving touch and tenderness. I walked up to him, hugged him tenderly and kissed him. I remembered last Saturday perfectly and I saw it as a breakthrough in my interactions with male energy. I was curious whether the dance floor would connect us today, or actually I wasn't curious, I was just waiting. I'd been looking forward to it since Friday evening.

Yes, tribal rhythms call me every Friday about twenty-four hours before the 5Rhythms class and won't even let me sleep. When this happens, I turn on music and dance with my whole body and soul.

When I enter the empty and still-dark 5Rhythms studio first, I smell its scent and experience excitement that makes it difficult for me to remain calm. A pleasant tension takes over me, as if not hundreds or even thousands, but millions of colourful butterflies fluttered in my chest. I feel a kind of elation, as if my wings, still glued to my body, were trying to gently stretch and greatly wanted to flutter. A little afraid of what might happen if they become so strong that they can lift me into the air, I say to myself softly: "Not yet, my dear. Let's wait."

My spirit is also lifted by the wave of love for Fulvio I've allowed to flow freely again. I start to warm up my body, trying to find and maintain balance. This allows me to ground myself in the here and now. Curious about what will happen today and what I will experience, I start my tribal dance. I focus on individual parts of my body one by one, reminding myself that I have feet, knees, hips, spine, elbows and hands. It's incredible that this can only be truly tuned into by practicing certain forms of mindfulness. It's strange how much we take our bodies for granted, and only pay attention to our body when it hurts.

I take the first step with my bare foot on the wooden parquet. My toes feel every irregularity in the floor. The wooden floor, reciprocating eacj touch, allows me to fully feel my body. I celebrate individual movements. First, I touch it with my toes and the ball of my foot, then I slide my heel over it, and finally I hug my entire foot to the floor.

Our instructor, Tomas, encourages us to experiment and make some non-obvious moves. So I start with the heel and end with the tip of the little toe.

"Remember that you also have knees" he reminds us.

Yes, knees. Did I pay attention to them two months ago? It's amazing that you can feel every fascia, every muscle surrounding this so-called royal joint.

We also have hips - a storehouse of our fears, built-in limitations and shame. That's power! When you give up control, when you allow yourself freedom, it turns out that you can move parts of you that you had no idea about.

The spine. Always stiff and upright, keeping your body ready for action. Why are you afraid to bend over? “Do not slouch! Stand up straight!” Do those words ring a bell? I heard them my entire childhood. Why did it matter that I stood up straight? I believe it had much less with posture, and more with a metaphorical meaning. Straight - correct, appropriate and perfect. By changing the shape of your body, do you become a different person? No, not to yourself, but it certainly changes the perception of you as a member of society.

Although we talk about Sparta's social philosophy as if it were the ancient past, the cult of what is ideal, flawless and doesn’t deviate from the norm is still deeply embedded in us. If you are different, society will quickly marginalize you. We don't like difference. I would say even more - we are afraid of it. Anything different shakes our sense of security and arouses fear. We feel afraid that everything we considered truths, norms and dogmas will collapse and we will no longer have anything to rely on.

We recoil from the exclusion in words like “hunchbacked” “bald” “invalid.” But there is another exclusionary word, although it appears milder at first. The word “strange”. You think differently - you are strange; you dress differently - you are strange; you behave differently - you are strange.

WEIRD – DIFFERENT – DANGEROUS

What I love about this dance technique is that it encourages you to find the courage to be yourself.

As one of my sisters in this practice said:

“I come here for the truth. I come here for the truth about myself and I find it. Thank you so much!”

I am also discovering the truth about myself. I peel off subsequent layers of my hard shell, and beneath them I see a brilliant and sensitive being, full of compassion for human frailty. An ethereal, tempting woman with a huge appetite for life. I am no longer ashamed of my sexuality and my needs.

The dance floor captivates me. On it, I am a child stamping my feet and shouting my anger, a wild woman dancing around the fire and a nymph sharing the light and warmth of touch.

I love dancing with my wild sisters and delicate brothers. I love those moments when one cry is followed by another, as if we were calling to each other from a distance or as if we were confirming our fealty to a brotherhood of souls.

It's amazing what strength comes from being in a group of such open people. The bravery you develop when you know that you're safe to be yourself. Truly yourself.

My newfound sensitivity no longer allows me to stand indifferently when I see one of the brothers in our meditation tribe crying. He suffers from paralysis of his legs and arms after a car accident. He looks so moved, that without hesitation, I walk up to him, sit behind his back and wrap my arms around his chest. His heart is beating like the piston of a speeding locomotive whose furnace is being stoked by the driver. This fuel is emotions. The courage to stand in your truth and say what has been hidden. The emotion of the unity of hearts and souls that unites our tribe. Gratitude for attention and acceptance. The locomotive accelerates even more. I hug him even tighter to ensure he knows he is not alone.

I had no idea that opening my heart to love would change me so profoundly.

I'm no longer indifferent when I walk past a drunk man with a bloodied nose who has fallen and is trying to pick up scattered beer cans and cigarettes. I ask how I can help him and clean up the blood with a napkin. I carefully collect all his belongings and pack them into the spacious pockets of his jacket. Two beers in one pocket, vanilla cheese, a pack of cigarettes, and a promotional leaflet in the other.

"This will be better" I say. "Now, you won't lose anything."

I help him get back on his feet and walk him home.

* * *

I love driving. I listen to my favorite music, admire the landscape, and greet other drivers. There is one thing I have a hard time with when driving. I don't know about you, but when I travel, I will spot every single truck carrying animals to the slaughterhouse. I can't help but imagine their fear and pain. In such situations, I also do what I feel. I feel pain for them, hug them all to my heart, and apologize.

* * *

Yesterday, while walking along Marszałkowska Street, I noticed a homeless woman sitting under a tree in a small folding chair. A flock of wild pigeons was running around her, waiting for a meal.

I walked over and asked if everything was okay? Could I get her anything?

"No, thank you" she replies. "I'm making coffee" she added and showed me a travel water boiling set.

The face of being whom life has not spared from suffering emerges from under the hood of a winter jacket. However, despite thobvious signs of a difficul life, her eyes still sparkle.

"She has nothing" some might say. Yes,she has no home, no job, doesn't even have a change of jacket, but in her eyes there is verything that is moportant: love, warmth, joy and hope.

"You have beautiful eyes" I said.

She smiled shyly.

"Can I take a photo of you?" I add.

"Sure, no problem."

I crouched down next to her, brought my head closer to hers and…

I posted our photo on my FB profile with the caption:

"Maybe homeless. Maybe poor. Maybe without opportunity.
Still a person. Same as you and me.
A sincere smile. Hope in her eyes. A verve for life!"

* * *

When I dance, I also learn the truth about others. About men's rebellion against their own sensitivity and women's denial of their own strength and courage. I am lucky because the energy of falling in love gives me the power to center myself in my truth.

I approach my tribemates closely, I touch them with tenderness, I am happy when they also touch me. I love dancing with them in pairs, threes and larger groups. I see how much we need acceptance, tenderness and love. I am nourished by the sense of brotherhood and community with people who are looking for the same thing in life as me - their authenticity.

When the last rhythms of tribal music fade away, I lie next to Tomas. His head touches my stomach, my legs hug his body, and our entangled hands hold us in an embrace of respect and trust. Every breath I take lifts his head, every breath he takes lifts our hands.

We feel.

I'm happy. My joyful laughter emerges from deep within. The laughter of a free and wild creature.

"Who likes closeness?" Asks our guide. Many people raise their hands.

"There are so many of you, eager for closeness" he says. "Ask yourself this question: Why do I only see a few couples connected to each other on this dance floor?" As he says this, he sprays the wonderful scent of moxa around the room, which envelops us.

There is silence.

The rhythms of music take us into unknown spaces of body and mind.

The lesson I learned is: Don't be afraid to be yourself.

The lesson you learned is:

Pushing My Boundries

I feel like he's still pushing me. Just when I think I've reached the limits of my patience and I can't take it anymore, Fulvio talks even less the next day. To survive it, I become like an elastic.

I take a few deep breaths, close my eyes and observe all the emotions coming to me.

I welcome:

- anger because I'm not getting what I want;
- annoyance because he is not what I want him to be;
- resentment because I don't feel respected;
- rejection because he doesn't pay enough attention to me.

I look at them, experience and verify each one individually. I look for moments in my life history that I can connect them with, when I felt the same way. Sometimes I see an image of me as a little girl, resentful of my parents when they did not pay attention to me. Other times I'm a teenager angry that my mom is reading my diary. My memory also reminds me of situations in which I felt rejected by my peers.

So I confront my emotions, which is not easy, but it's the only way to truly dethaw our full self.

I'm starting tapping therapy.

"What is that?" You ask. It's the common name of the EFT technique, or Emotional Freedom Technique - an emotional freedom technique that involves tapping selected points on the body while repeating words describing the emotions we cannot cope with.

Its aim is to neutralize what hurts us, what blocks us and takes away our strength. Every negative emotion or traumatic experience that we do not work through stays inside us like dust, and maybe even forms a shell around us. Tapping allows us to get rid of this shell that cuts us off from life.

I keep breathing deeply and repeating loudly:

"Even though I'm mad at Fulvio... I love and respect myself."

Depending on my mental condition, my tapping practice lasts from a few seconds to several minutes. When all difficult emotions settle within me and I achieve inner peace, I set new rules of the game by telling myself:

"What was yesterday is no longer relevant! The rules have changed! Today is a new day!"

Then I let love, understanding, longing and the energy of falling in love into my heart. And they do the rest.

* * *

The weekend is coming up. I hear promises again that Fulvio will call in the evening, but - as my sister says ironically - "he doesn't say which evening."

On Monday, he just apologizes for not calling.

There is a deafening silence on Tuesday.

On Wednesday, he sends a "good morning" and schedules an online date, which he later cancels because he's at the office.

He also cancels our date on Thursday because he's working late. On Friday, "good morning" and then silence until Monday. Today is Wednesday - no contact.

Why do I put up with this?

- Maybe to test my own patience?
- Maybe to confront the humiliation?
- Maybe to get to know my pride and arrogance better, who don't like it when someone goes against their expectations?
- Maybe to observe my anger and learn to control it?
- Maybe it's a training in coming to terms with the fact that you can't always have what you want?
- Maybe to test my confidence in life?
- Maybe to respect people regardless of whether they act according to my plan?

What do I think?

- He only likes me and that's OK.
- He wants to meet me for some good sex. Maybe we'll be better off as just lovers.
- He likes to be with me when he has space for me.

You ask what pushing my boundaries means to me?

- Leaving the comfort zone.
- Expanding my limits, including the limits of patience.
- Abandoning predictability to feel alive every day.
- Getting to know myself by observing how far I can go, how much I can do.
- Immersing mysefl in a full range of emotions.
- Being ready to thaw my defenses, no matter what that brings.
- Following what calls to me, without fear.
- Defying stereotypes.
- Doing what I feel, regardless of the consequences.

In our next therapy session, Julia asks:
“What are you plans now that he’s not really communicative?”

"He contacted me on Thursday and I wrote him a letter, but I haven't sent it yet" I tell her. "I wrote how I'm feeling. I thanked him for the weekend in Bologna... and it's actually this letter that I want to talk to you about."

"Okay, but let's tackle that later" she says. "I'd like to focus on what is between the two of you. In my opinion, the way you communicate looks like lovers' conversations. Once you lose joy in what you have, it won't happen anymore. What unites you should be built on the goodness of your experiences, not on what overwhelms you. Lovers who are having an affair, don't see their wife or husband as an obstacle to their affair. What will happen down the road depends on whether you continue to fall in love or focus on what is bothering you about each other."

I'm speechless…

"This is a completely new perspective for me" I tell her. "I have never looked at the relationship between a man and a woman this way."

"Of course" she says. "You've never looked it this way because our society recognizes only people who live in monogamous nuclear families, it doesn't grant lovers the right to exist."

I want so badly to push past my boundaries, to grow so much that I can truly feel calm as I wait for news from him, hen be sincerely happy when he writes, but I can't get there yet.

My anxiety tells me to sort this out and gain clarity at any cost. On the heels of anxiety come thoughts like: "Give him an ultimatum. Make him choose!" Fear. What a nasty fellow.

* * *

Yesterday I went to the cinema to see a Polish- made movie called "Girls to Buy." Reviews are calling it skinemax, a weak movie with low energy.

I'm sure that before my transformation I would have felt the same way, but now I don't see any soft-core porn when I watch it. I see a film about difficult love and women who dream of freedom and independence. I was not scandalized by the topic of human trafficking. I just saw the story of women trying to find their way in the world.

I cried after leaving the cinema. I felt so sorry for all these women. I was filled with great compassion, respect and wistfulness. I also felt grateful that I had done the work and could now freely experience such emotions. After the tears came laughter, and then I just kept laughing and crying.

The lesson I learned is: Opening up to emotions is life changing.

The lesson you learned is:

....
....
....
....
....
....
....
....
....
....
....
....
....
....
....
....
....
....
....
....
....
....
....
....
....
....
....
....

Respect

"I know he has something to teach me. But how to learn this lesson and not go crazy?"

Julia sighed and began to explain:

"Iwona, understand that this guy may not respond to you. Why? He wants to reply when on his terms. The more secret feelings a man has for you, the more difficult it is for him to write. Some people function this way. Your style of communication is sending frequent messages and replying immediately. Your perception is that when you write, he "must" respond. Understand that he may have a different communication style. Maybe he needs to work up to it? Maybe writing doesn't come to him naturally? People need the freedom to reach out to us whenever they want. We know your guy has depth, and if that's true, he experiences life more deeply. A person who experiences things deeply will take a word and think about it, and when no words come to inspired this thinking, there is also no answer."

"Yeah. Respect for people is giving them space, letting go of control" I sighed.

"A question for you: what should you do to feel better in this situation and in this mix of communication styles?" Julia asks. "Listen: good ol' mom and pop would talk about everything and everyone all the time. If we accept the theory that in every relationship there is a limited number of words to say, then if you talk through everything at the beginning of your relationship, it is no wonder that after a few years people no longer have anything to say to each other. Everyone sits in their chair as if hypnotized and nothing happens."

"True. They become two people who have completely lost interest. In themselves and more" I interjected.

"Now let's talk about your Italian" she says. "Consider how busy he is and how he has to mobilize himself to have deep conversations with you. If he has the depth I think he has, then his friendships and loves will last forever because they are run much deeper than words. Listen to what he says, not what he doesn't say. Do you remember how replied to your letter?"

"What letter?"

The one you sent after returning from Bologna.

Oh, yes, that letter…

The Letter to Fulvio

Fulvio, you know I'm in love with you, and I hope you feel and see it.

I feel like a teenager in love, but I'm 54 years old, I know myself and I know that it's not just a temporary infatuation. Those were wonderful moments – with you in Bologna. Yes, I was a little shy and a little withdrawn because I wasn't sure how we'd feel spending time together. Truthfully I was most unsure about how you'd feel spending time with me. I was afraid that what I felt for you would turn out to be too much for you. So I thought it would be better if I took a proverbial "cold shower" and cooled down a bit before leaving. I think this is normal at the beginning of every relationship, especially one where you feel butterflies in your stomach from the very first moments. So I cooled down my emotions (which wasn't easy because I'm very emotional) and I'm glad I only cooled them down and didn't freeze them, because thanks to that I had a wonderful weekend with you.

The two months of waiting to see you were very difficult, but also pleasant. They were difficult because I missed you so much; I wasn't sure if you would want to see me; I was afraid that something would interrupt us at the last minute. They were also difficult because we had very little contact with each other. Yes, I know - you said I could write and call you whenever I wanted. My problem was that I could talk to you on the phone every day, but I was afraid that you would get tired of it. Why? Because I wasn't sure if I was as important to you as you were to me, and I didn't have the courage to ask you about it. I have never felt as intimidated by any man as I do with you.

In turn, these two months were pleasant because I lived in hope and every day I imagined our meeting at the airport, our motorbike ride and our sex. You set me on fire. I haven't felt as feminine as I do now for a long time.

Our weekend of, as you called it - "first times", was wonderful. I got many birthday gifts from you. Delightful sex, which I still miss. A motorcycle ride during which I felt both peace and excitement in one. I have already been a passenger on a motorcycle several times, but no driver led his machine as smoothly and with such sensitivity as you. A delicious dinner at an Italian pizzeria and homemade spaghetti cooked by you. It's very nice that you asked your friend to show us a bit of Bologna. Thank you for letting me meet your friends from the foundation. I can still feel the wind in my hair and the smile on my face during our crazy scooter rally. We were so happy and carefree then. You must admit that we managed really well as two people on a single-person scooter. We really make a good couple. Apart from a few mishaps: an almost destroyed garage door, the plague of hearts on the balcony and the fact that I stubbornly slept on your half of the bed all night and that I can't understand why you don't have a hair dryer. I consider this time a happy one and I can't wait to do it again.

However, the greatest birthday gift I received from you were your words: "You are my girl" and "I love you" and your reaction when I said that I love you. At that moment you squeezed my hand so tightly and a happy smile appeared on your face that no other words were needed.

I feel happy when you smile at me. I love the way you look at me. Your "Hi, my sweet" and "Hi, honey" are as sweet to me as chocolate gelato.

I'm very attracted to you. I miss the touch of your hands and the embrace of your arms. I love it when you touch me as if by accident - when you open the car door for me, when you put my helmet on and put your hand on my knee while I'm riding a motorcycle. I'm crazy about your hairy chest. I want to melt my thighs into yours. I love your whole body. When I make love to you, I experience true ecstasy. I would like more and more and more...

With you I feel such stillness and inner peace that I don't need words. I don't have to say anything. I just want to be with you, here and now. Your energy envelops me, and the sound of your voice is like wonderful music. I enjoy your sense of humor. I am inspired by your passions and interests. I am happy lying lazily next to you on the couch. My dream way to relax is to take a walk with you or watch rugby matches together. I love watching you cook, how you set the table for dinner, how you carefully arrange your things in the garage. I'm proud of you for being able to help people as selflessly as you helped that crying woman from the Marconi Express. You are a charming and warm man with a big heart.

To me, you are not one of a million men, you are one in a million.

Because I feel so good with you, I wanted to give us a chance to develop our relationship. I wanted to fly to you every 2-3 weeks just to make us happy. It would definitely be lovely to have time for us, a bit of relaxation that each of us needs, and a way to get to know each other better.

I'm not looking for a husband, I don't need a man's money or a home. I'm not looking for a sponsor. I am looking for a partner with whom I will spend my free weekends, celebrate the most important days in our lives and go on little holidays with him. I want to share some of my passions with him, to go for walks and listen to music. I want to see how happy he is when he can fulfill his goals. I would like a man to stand by my side, so that I can stand by his side as we enjoy life together. I want to see the joy of our meetings in his eyes, feel his interest in me and my life, and feel that he misses me when I'm not there.

I'm very curious as to what you want. This is a great mystery to me. We've never talked about it before. I'm sure I could understand you better if I knew what you were looking for and what you expected. What kind of relationship with a woman do you need and what does "being a couple" mean to you? I would like us to talk honestly about your needs and what is important to you. How do you imagine a relationship with me and where is my place in your life... It's up to you. Nobody can dictate to you how to live your life. Your honesty will give me a chance to address this situation and to make an informed decision.

It would be great if we could, with full confidence, not only be able to, but also want to write to each other and talk to each other openly about our feelings, about what we are afraid of, what annoys us and what makes us happy. If you told me all this, it would help me to get rid of the fear and uncertainty that lives inside of me.

I don't want to pretend that everything is fine, just like I couldn't pretend that I returned to Poland with a smile on my face. I cried at the airport, on the plane and on the train returning to Warsaw. I wept many tears. Multiple passengers asked me what happened and if they could help me in any way. A young man on the train said to me: "Don't worry, everything will be okay."

And that's who I am, darling. I have deep emotions and I don't want to hide them. I want to talk about my concerns. Hiding emotions leads to withdrawal or anger, and no relationship can grow like that.

Yes I am afraid. Of what? I'm afraid of losing you because I don't know you. It is very easy to lose your way in a maze of guesses and assumptions. Secrets and misdirections do not help maintain a balance in a relationship.

You are a great mystery to me. You tell me that you miss me, that I am important to you, but there are days when you barely contact me. You say

I'm your girl, but you don't call me or write to me. I want you to know that this behavior makes me doubt whether you need me in your life at all. I don't know if it's just your nature? Maybe you don't trust me? Maybe you're afraid too?

It's difficult for me when I don't know your expectations and needs. I don't know what to think when I send you messages and you don't respond. I often wonder if what I do interests you at all. When you don't tell me anything about yourself and don't ask me anything, I wonder if you would notice if I disappeared.

Maybe you will answer: "Please, no, honey." Maybe you'll think that I'm hysterical or immature, but I'm writing what I feel.

Or maybe we just need an honest conversation, so that I can then say, write and do what I feel? Maybe you would also like to ask me some things? Maybe you also have your doubts, maybe they're stopping you from opening up to me? Maybe we are both lost in our own doubts? Maybe we both retreated into our shells and, like two-hundred-year-old turtles, lie motionless on the beach, waiting for the tide?

I get suspicious when you tell me that you are with your son and that you cannot write to me. I won't get jealous because that makes no sense, but your disappearance on weekends make me suspcious that you're meeting another woman, not your son. You disappear every Friday afternoon and remain silent.

Maybe you do spend your weekends with your son. Maybe it's with that woman Paola - who called you during my stay in Bologna - or maybe someone else...

Suspicions are born when I'm with you and your phone rings and rings and rings and you won't answer it, can't or won't pick up and say "Hey. I'm with Iwona and we're having dinner" but instead you leave to another room to talk.

Suspicions are born when you tell me that you love me, that you miss me and that I am important to you, but you keep dodging my offer to visit you in December.

Sometimes I get the impression that you're trying to provoke me into saying: "Fulvio, I don't feel important to you, I don't feel respected by you. It's over" .

My dear, I wrote what I feel in the hope that it will help us. If you don't want to, you don't have to explain anything to me.

I understand perfectly well that my freedom ends where yours begins.

That letter never reached Bologna.

"Why?" – you ask.

I do not know.

I wrote a shorter message and received the following reply:

> "Hello my sweet. Thank you for your message. I have no secrets. There is no one standing in our way. I have no other romantic relationships except the one I have with you. You've just met me during a very difficult time in my work and in my life, when I have a lot to do. It was a pleasure spending time with you. It will always be a pleasure for me to be with you. Call me if you want. I'm home now. Kisses."

I think the paradox of human relationships is that while it is very easy for us to pay respects to strangers, it is much more difficult for us to do so with those who are closest to us.

When you feel like someone is disrespecting you, what does it mean? Are you seeing disrespectful behaviour, or is it actually your own suspicion and disrespect of others activated instead?

When Fulvio says he will call in the morning, he means his morning, not my morning. Would I like to talk about serious topics at 6:00 am? Well, I could at any time - that's a hangover I still have from being a corporate workhorse and an incurable people pleaser regardless of the price I pay for it. Today I know that this morning I should focus on my rituals: exercise, breakfast and getting ready for work, and not on serious Polish-Italian conversations.

I can't expect people to drop everything any time I have a question. I can't measure people by my own yardstick. Everyone has the right to have their goals and their own ways of going about things.

Just a moment ago I was feeling what it's like to be under pressure to communicate. My business bombarded me with over ten emails. Bombarded me? Yes. It certainly felt like it.

I was still at home, but my head was already at work. I was trying to prepare breakfast, pack my laptop, not forget the laptop charger, remember my phone, notebook and glasses, without which I can no longer work. Ha, ha. She was siting in an office chair, with her head full of creative juices, sending messages.

In the past, I would have dropped everything and started answering her questions. Of course I would be late for work or I wouldn't get to eat breakfast. Why? Because I would have to fire up my laptop, consider the questions she is asking about, and give a sensible answer.

What did I do this time?

The discomfort I felt made me realize just in time that pressure stiffens us, makes us anxious and even irritated.

Before my eyes appeared a vision of Fulvio, "running" nervously at the notification of my message.

I remember once writing to him resentfully:

- You didn't even text me "hello" today.
- Yes, because I've been working since 6:00 am.
- Yes, but that one "hello" would only take you five seconds.
- Honey, but for these five seconds, I have to completely cut my-

self off from my work, reset myself, to be present in what I'm writing to you, and then it's not five seconds anymore.

What is my lesson here?

Stable people respond when they have time. I don't want to fall into old patterns. I need to give myself and others a chance to think about the answer, not to answer before the question is finished, not to answer automatically. I don't have to answer right away.

The lack of a single text message when I need it should not spoil my joy in life and everything I have experienced. Just because someone doesn't immediately do what I want doesn't mean they don't respect me. They just need their space.

The lesson I learned is: Give people the space to live life on their own terms - including yourself.

The lesson you learned is:

Did I Ask for This?

"My dear, I would like you to examine something" Julia said. "I want you to look at it carefully. Fulvio came into your life with an energy of someone taking care of his business. The universe put an independent man on your path. A man who is balanced, who knows what he wants and goes for it, who is "fully himself". He is showing you all of the energies and feelings you have asked for. When you look at it, you see: freedom, independence, taking care of business.

Remember how you prayed to the universe to meet a man you would love? You also asked for a man who would allow you to be independent. You wanted to create your own life and have agency over your decisions. A few weeks ago you said that you wanted to have time to open your business and create something. You also dreamed of having space for yourself and your development."

I watched in disbelief as Julia's words came together into one coherent whole and created a neon sign with the inscription: "FREEDOM" before my eyes.

Meanwhile, Julia continued:

"Now you can have it all. This man is offering freedom, and as a bonus, it gives you the promise of joy, because you are sure that you will feel joy every time you meet. Honey, you got what you asked for!"

There was a moment of silence.

Did I ask for this? I scan my thoughts and desires that I had expressed over the past months.

Damn it! Yes it's true! My words spoken in July echoed in my head. "God, I would love to be able to look at my man with pleasure. I dream of nothing else but to look into his eyes and feel love."

OK, so I have that… Fulvio - a boy-wonder whom I can stare at for hours, who hypnotizes me so much that whatever he does - or rather in his case, whatever he does not do, because he does very little, you even argue he does nothing. I'm not angry at him, or I'm only angry for a moment. I think about him with tenderness and am full of understanding.

"It's not easy, but I am extremely grateful for all these experiences. I don't want a clingy man who will smother me. I don't want to be his nanny, mother or domestic help."

"Exactly" Julia echoed.

"I have my hobbies, I like spending time with my friends and I also love being by myself" I went on. "I think that a great partner for me is an independent man who also has his own hobbies and his own life. Theoretically, my Italian is perfect. We could spend holidays together and visit each other from time to time in Poland or Italy. With him I could be an independent woman. The only thing I'm missing is... Well... while everything sounds great in theory, in practice it's different. Especially when you're in love. Falling in love is beautiful, but it's not easy. When I'm in love, I'm vulnerable because I'm more sensitive to all emotions. It's even more difficult when you fall in love with someone who is far from you and even if you want to, you can't be with him. Then even missing that "good morning" at the start of the day can throw you off your rhythm.

"Sounds right to me" interjected Julia.

"So when it comes to self-transformation, the work is full-on, with no protections and all options set to highest difficulty, yeah?" I chuckle. "I can't deny that the feeling of falling in love makes me braver. I feel so strong that while in it I don't worry about anything. There's a chance that my job may disappear in November, and I'm cool as a cucumber about it. Thanks to this feeling, hardly anything can scare me anymore. "Nobody can break my stride" as Matthew Wilder once sang. I have never felt such peace before."

"Being open to feelings can monumentally change us" Julia says. "You got what you asked for. You wanted to be independent - you are. You wanted time to take care of your own affairs and to create - you have it.

Do you remember how you felt when your previous beau, Alessandro, offered to visit you every month for two weeks so you could spend part of the month together?"

"Yes" I answer. "I was going to work when the message came, I was relaxed and cheerful and suddenly - his offer. It really hit me like a ton of bricks. I don't know why, but I was terrified. I couldn't explain it, I just felt it and my first thought was, 'Oh god! This guy is going to invade my wonderful life.' It hadn't occurred to me before. It was a spontaneous reaction, real."

"You asked for independence, that's what you go. So now get to it and use it. Do all the things that nourish you, that will build your independence, treat the company of a man as a pleasant bonus. An unexpected gift that you will enjoy immensely. The world is challenging you to fulfill your own purpose, to create your own creation, and if you don't step up, if you don't celebrate happiness after returning from paradise, everything will stop happening. If you'd like to plan your next trip, plan it.. Not on the principle of acting on your whims and wants, but on the principle of letting fate take you to unexpected places. You know, when someone asks 'how soon can we meet?' and the other person replies 'in three months' you have to acknowledge that's their reality."

"The hardest thing for me is the waiting. For his reply, for him to send a proactive message, for his call."

"WAITING" Julia repeated bluntly. "You can't be in this space. The energy of waiting is the same as the energy of wanting. Fixating on something is not the best way to gain it.That energy is so powerful that it will stay with you and engulf you. That's why you have to let go. The only way to fight the energy of wanting is to let go. It's the same with waiting. Once you start waiting, you will wait forever. Instead, get grounded in your life's reality! Look at where you are in life. You can stare at the photos of your loved one for hours at a time if you like, at his wonderful eyes. See it for the gift that it is."

"The universe is beautifully showing me my next difficult lesson" I said. "I have excellent relationships with men with whom I am not in love. I can talk to them honestly and with respect, I with them I feel grounded and strong in my feminine power. Fulvio shows me that when I fall in love I lose my sense of balance... I am sure that if Fulvio had showed as much interest in me as Alessandro, and if he invited me to Italy, I would drop my who whole life and all of the success I've built for myself, I'd jump on the magic flying carpet of love and…"

"And then what?"

"Then I would be dependent on a man again. I would be in a new country without knowing the language or knowing anyone. The process of quitting on myself, of hiding my own ambition, desires and unfulfilled dreams would begin. Would I give up my self in the name of love? Would I give up on loving myself for the sake of loving a man? Yes, that's who I am. Fulvio is like a mirror showing me all of this. At the bottom of it all, I am grateful to him with all my heart for being the way he is. Even keeled and keeping me at a distance. I have to learn to love without giving up on myself, without prior expectations and requirements, without building a shell of inaccessibility around myself."

Look how far I have come, I think to myself. Just a few months ago, the ideal man for you could only be a down-to-earth alpha-male businessman who would guarantee you stability and security, on whose shoulder you could always lean. Who knows how quickly you'd realize that you no longer go to pottery classes because on Fridays he wants to go to the cottage. You would betray your dance tribe in favor of a boat ride or a trip to the mountains. Do you see it?

What would happen if you were working on your business on Sunday and some Dan or Steve told you: "Don't work on a Sunday, rest, come over for dinner. I will give you everything you need."

How would you feel when he'd eventually say to you:

"Don't be so difficult."

"I don't want to fall in love, falling in love is too complicated. It's enough for me that I like a woman and that she turns me on."

"You expect too much from life. You can't have everything."

"What's the point of all this lovey-dovey nonsense anyway? You're not a teenager. It's just making life messy."

"I can give you everything. What else are you looking for?"

"Who's whispering in your ear?" Julia says. "It is your ego, trying to travel well worn paths again. Sometimes one word is worth more than thousands."

"When Fulvio writes to me in the morning, it puts me in a great modd for the entire day" I tell her.

"He may feel the same way. Your one voice message may be enough for him for the whole day. You have to choose. If you are in love with him, examine what you're getting from this feeling, and see if you want to give it up for the sake of having more communication. Or do you prefer to hear fewer words, but a man who keeps you rooted in feeling the energy of being in love?" Julia drops this important question at my feet.

"You've told me that you believe that when you think about a man, it means that he is actually thinking about you. Then follow that concept through to its natural conclusion. If you are thinking about him a dozen times a day, it must mean that he's thinking about you a dozen times a day. So he is emotionally with you. OK, he's not a prolific writer or communicator, but he thinks about you often. You can't walk around saying you believe this truth about intuiting someone else thinking about you, but also not believe it at the same time. Look, here is a wave of love mixed with independence you were waiting for, it's a wave you should surf. And you either want to live according to your truth, or you need to shut things down. But if I can give you one piece of advice, don't rush your decision. Focus on what people say to you, not to the things they haven't said" She continues. "Anyway, where is the formula for how many words must be spoken or written to prove that you love someone? Remember all the love letters we wrote in our youth that led to nothing?"

"Yes it's true. My time with Fulvio has taken me down completely new paths" I tell her. "Falling in love has awoken the most sensitive strings of my heart and soul. I've discovered sensitivity that I had no idea about, and activated my creativity and courage. Even the fears that accompany this love are not so scary when I can see them from a different perspective. I am grateful that I have learned so much about myself and that I am more aware of what I still have to work through. I love myself more and more. Once upon a time, such a relationship would have destroyed me. I would go mad and sink into the abyss of resentment and regret. Now I am transforming myself so that I can enjoy what I get from life.

The lesson I learned is: Use the gifts you get.

The lesson you learned is:

Life Is a University

I'm on a video call about my first book.

"How are you feeling, darling?" Asks my colleague, Gosia.

"I feel the way I look. You know I have COVID. But my heart is also broken, because my relationship with Fulvio has probably ended."

"What happened?"

"Well, on Monday, I sent my boyfriend a photo of myself that my sister took during a FaceTime conversation, and that unleashed a huge storm. Or rather, a deathly silence.

Two days later, a missive arrived from Bologna.

"I'd like to know who's the lucky guy you're talking to on FaceTime who's taking pictures of you?" I was so confused. A moment later I received my photo with a green arrow pointing to my interlocutor's window. Yep. My man was convinced that he's not the only man I have FaceTime calls with. He didn't even consider that it could be someone other than a man. On the one hand, it was surprising that a man who won't talk to me for three days at a time can be jealous of me. But, of course he has the right to feel how he feels. He has the right to be jealous of a woman who told him she loved him. He has the right to feel rejected and cheated by a woman who misses him and might be dating another man. He has the right to feel how he feels.

I kept calling him to try and explain the situation, but he stung by an unexpected romantic rejection, wouldn't answer. I recorded a message explaining the whole situation, but it went unanswered."

"How are you feeling now?" my friend asks.

"Part of me can't believe that things could possibly end like this. It's such a stupid situation! The other part is afraid that anything is possible."

"You're afraid? What of?"

"Oh you know, that I will lose the man I love, to whom I am so attracted that no other man can interest me. That I will lose love."

"Are you feeling anything else?" Gosia continues her questions.

"Feeling guilty that I sent that photo. I didn't see any of this coming."

"Is there anything good that can come out of this situation? The inner work you've been doing will say that this is not a coincidence. Everything happens for a reason. Right?"

"Yes, I know it's not a coincidence. The one good thing that has happened is that finally told Fulvio about my feelings, with complete honesty and without fear. I told him what I was previously afraid to say because I didn't want to overwhelm him or smother him. In the recording, I explained the situation with the photo and added that it was a simple misunderstanding. He still didn't respond, so I sent him another voice message.

> "Every morning I wait for a message from you, every evening I wait for a message from you. I miss you and I love you, and you know it. I wanted to visit you in November, I want to visit you in December. I told you that I am willing to travel every three weeks because I want to be with you, not because I have some other guy. Fuck. If you remember correctly, I wanted to post our photo on FB because I don't have any secrets. My boyfriend from Bologna is not a problem for me.

All of my friends and family know about you. All of my friends know that I want to spend New Year's Eve with you and that I am waiting, still waiting for your invitation. Also, please; don't make a whore out of me! I did a lot of things with you because I love you, not because I'm some slut. OK, sometimes I get outlandish ideas, but don't ever treat me like a whore. I'm fifty-four years old and I have clear rules. Why don't you tell me when I'm welcome back in Italy? I look forward to it. I fell in love with you at first sight in Bologna, on our first date. This feeling for you inspires me and makes me happy. Yes, it's also painful because you have so little time for me. You don't call, you don't write. You're always busy. I wait without complaint. I'm waiting for you to have more time for me, I'm waiting because I don't want to inconvenience you, I know your life is different than mine. I'm a free woman. Yes, I am a free woman, but I have a boyfriend in Bologna. I miss you and I love you and I am not a whore. I can only imagine how shocked you must have been when you thought I could be cheating on you. I can imagine the pain you felt, but the worst thing we could do, knowing that this was a misunderstanding, is not to talk about it."

"Maybe some other good things could come out of this?"

"Maybe I'll get to know him better?" I ponder.

"Okay, what other good things could you take out of getting to know him better?"

"That we will become closer to each other. As long as he stops being mad at me."

"What if he stays offended to his dying day?"

"Well, then he wasn't the guy for me."

"I think this is the point, my darling…" says Gosia. "The Universe is giving you a chance to look at Fulvio not only through a lover's eyes, but also sensibly, to see that he is not only amazing and wonderful, but also jealous, easily offended and prone to anger. In other words, he's just human. This stage of really getting to know your loved one is one of the stages of falling in love. Every couple should go through it... The universe is showing you what you need to work on. I think that your soul subconsciously asked for this situation, to either bring you closer together or truly tear you apart. Your soul knows how difficult and tiring it is for you to not know where you stand. I think it's a good thing that this happened, and right now. Your illness, the misunderstanding with the photo, his reaction. Some small war was needed to break or strengthen this relationship."

"How high is your fear of losing Fulvio? On a scale of one to ten." She adds.

"Ten!" I answer. "For example, this morning I had a feeling that this situation make me unable to finish writing my book."

"It's a life test."

"Today, when Fulvio wrote to me, I was proofreading, and when I read his message, I thought: 'Shit, should I throw this book in the trash? I'm including unflattering details about him in it, like that he's quick to get offended. This book will end up in his hands one day and that will be the end of us. Then I looked at the words I had written and said to mysel: 'No way. I'm definitely publishing this book!'"

* * *

It's the third day of my COVID self-isolation and I'm going through a crisis. Fulvio promised to call me tomorrow. Only that tomorrow never comes. In a hoarse voice, I recorded a message:

"Gosia, you asked me how I'm feeling. I miss him so much. This illness has robbed me of my strength and made me feel terrible. I've lost all my previous self-confidence. Just now, once again, I found myself thinking about leaving this book and not writing it. Unbelievable. There's a buzzing in my head: 'What's the point. Who will read this? It's juvenile to write about your life, you'll only embarrass yourself! But this is all mixed up Fulvio. I can see it. When he writes to me, I have energy, and when he doesn't, I simply fade away. I have to... I would like to find a way to not be on such a rollercoaster. He called me yesterday and I had so much fun. Today there's no contact at all and I immediately feel depressed. I'll tell you that I have to cope somehow, but it's really difficult. This is bad, I feel it. I'm addicted to his attention. His contact with me, even one stupid "buongiorno" gives me peace. I cannot function without it. I don't know, maybe you have some advice, my dear? Because I can't take it much longer. (I start crying). I feel myself losing strength. I'm exhausted. I'm catastrophizing again. That he'll leave me, that he's bored of me, and so on and so on. I was already so far into my therapy, or rather, I thought I had already processed so much, and it seemed to me that I had some distance from his behavior. And today I see that I have no distance and that I was fooling myself. The universe has come again and shown me exactly where I am. I should have a healthy distance to the situation. Meanwhile, my healthy distance is wondering some prairie, and I'm in Warsaw. Today I just saw exactly how much I'm able to distance myself from him. I'm not. I have no distance. All it takes is for him to be silent for one day and my distance simply falls to pieces. These are my emotions today..."

"Iwonka, what is happening with Fulvio now is the most important thread in this whole book!

Look!

Falling in love.

Falling in love – what does it truly mean? You already know that it's about delving deeper into self-love, working through personal challenges. Yet, there's also the undeniable pull of chemistry. That magnetic attraction to a man so intense, you can't envision your life without him. It's intoxicating, like a potent drug. And why do I think that what is happening now is the most important thread of your book? Remember how you once said that relationships mirror our deepest truths? Right now, you're in the midst of a beautiful journey. Remember the void you felt after your last breakup? How insignificant you deemed yourself? Now, you've come full circle, but not without detours through darkness, despair, and unhealthy coping mechanisms. Like an alcoholic who might need a few tries at rehabilitation to overcome addiction. My dear, you're facing a déjà vu of sorts. If Fulvio doesn't talk to you, your life stops making sense. It's the perfect drug, but it's not real. You know that if it wasn't him, you'd have this same dynamic with someone else. Even if you don't end up with someone, you will still live a happy life. What should you do now? The same thing you did after your previous big break up .Seek the underlying truth. Part of this infatuation is an addiction you need to break free from. You might love him forever, or perhaps he was only supposed to take you so far and this is where his role ends? Ask yourself: How do I liberate myself from this dependence? Seek guidance from the angels, confront those drug-induced false beliefs head-on, and document them meticulously."

I stop the recording, take a piece of paper and a pen and write down the false beliefs:

- I will never find true love again.
- This is the only man I can love.
- Only he can give me pleasure and love.
- I won't be as comfortable with anyone else.
- When he leaves, I will lose the ability to love.
- Without him I will never feel such joy for life again.
- Without him, I will lose everything I have worked for.
- I will be incomplete without him.

I return to the recording, realizing that each of these sentences may be as true as it is irrational. Meanwhile, I hear Gosia's voice:

> "Now, can you spot the insight among these negative thoughts? This is the most valuable element in your therapy. The drug is back. The toxicity of the thoughts you wrote doesn't come from Fulvio, it comes from your mind!"

* * *

"What would you like to happen with all the emotions you have for Fulvio? Do you want to continue to love him harmoniously? Or something else?"

"I want to learn to love him harmoniously! Because that's the only path that will prove to me that my recovery is possible. If I can't navigate this while in the throes of my addiction, then when? I fear that if I give up now, any future romance will follow the same tumultuous path. The best option for me is to overcome the addiction while it is still alive. To face it head-on amidst the 'hunger' for Fulvio, not after a potential breakup. If I wait until we part ways, I might deceive myself into believing I'm cured. 'I'm free from addiction,' I'd say, but in truth, I would only be free from the feelings, not the underlying issue. The real victory lies in managing the addiction, not just escaping the object of my affection."

"My dear, that's the next stage of your journey. Try scripting manifestation, do tapping and meditation as you did in March."

My Future Script

I am grateful that I can love Fulvio with ease.
I am grateful to be a free and sober woman.
I am grateful that my relationship with Fulvio is mature and balanced, a source of joy and empowerment.
I am grateful that I can love maturely and deeply.
I am happy in every dimension of life with Fulvio. My happiness is overwhelming regardles of whether he is close or far away.
This has already happened. This has already happened. This has already happened. This has already happened.

"You're at university, and now it's time for you to become the professor."

The lesson I learned is: Life is a constant learning experience.

The lesson you learned is:

What For?

During our next conversation, Gosia asked:

"Darling, speak your mind. Why are you writing a book?"

I mentioned a few things in response:

- To cope with missing a man.
- To avoid emotions of anger and scorn.
- To describe what I felt when I fell in love.
- To illustrate my path in therapy during the period of falling in love.

"This book could not have been written if Fulvio had not come into my life. The painful part of falling in love led me to discover my love of writing."

"But why are you writing *this* book?"

Because I was triggered by things that I had no idea were a challenge for me. At this same time:

- I reconciled with my dad.
- I regained regard for men.
- I regained regard for humanity.
- I uncovered that it is difficult for me to be patient.
- I learned about my greatest fears.
- I entered the energy of fearlessness.
- I had the courage to do what I feel.

- I got my wings back.

I allowed myself to be pushed out of my comfort zone by my relationship with Fulvio. When I think I have reached the limits of my capabilities, he tightens the screws even more and it turns out that I can handle more. I am curious about how much more I can do while in the energy of being in love, and I am observing it."

"Why do you want to publish it?" she probed.

Even in my most beautiful dreams, the thought of writing a book was just a distant possibility, a whisper of an idea. Initially, my intent was to chronicle my therapy journey in a personal diary. However I realized that these words could evolve into a book, and I want to share it with other women to inspire them to:

- Embrace self-love in its purest form.
- Take pride in their femininity, celebrating its unique power and grace.
- Express their sexuality freely and without fear.
- Be free to speak their truths, their feelings and desires.
- Discard outdated, limiting beliefs that hold them back.
- Dispel the myth of "I could never."
- Gain a sense of freedom.
- Be open to the possibility of falling in love after fifty, regardless of the outcome.
- Give themselves permission to start a new life.
- Use courage to overcome fear.
- Approache every relationship with respect and intentionality.
- Allow themselves the gift of living a wonderful life at every moment.
- Celebrate life through the full spectrum of emotions, as they are the essence of our existence.
- Give themselves permission to fully experience life.

"Fascinating. You know, I believe that the changes that occurred in you while you were falling in love with Fulvio were primarily your work, and he was only a secondary participant."

"Maybe, maybe not" I responded. "I feel extremely grateful to him. I hope that women who read my book will notice that falling in love can be used to push yourself, to examine yourself and grow. It does not have to end with being immersed in rejection, anger and mutual accusations. No need to pronounce: "I will never fall in love again and I will never trust any man again! All men are pigs!"

"Exactly. It would be wonderful to start another relationship with an open and clear heart. Your transformation began some time ago in a tough way - with abandonment that made you consider ending your life. Then you went through self-love therapy with Alessandro. Then there was falling in love with Fulvio, which you used with intention to further transform yourself. Someone else in your position would have abandoned it long ago. They'd say, 'How long can you wait for a guy to call you? You don't want to talk to me? Get lost!' You didn't give up. You used every element that manifested itself in this relationship for your own transformation. To such an extent that you started to feel love and respect so strongly:

- for men,
- for humanity,
- for yourself,
- for the world,
- for life."

"My life since March has been like a great gift. I am so grateful for everything I had the opportunity to live and experience" I said. "Therapists say that the key to happiness for each of us is to love yourself. I agree with that. But I believe that we cannot truly love ourselves without respecting all people.

After my breakup in March, I quickly gained strength and regained my power... I was nothing could stop me, that I was strong, liberated and I didn't need anyone.

It was my relationship with Alessandro that showed me that only another person can show you how emotionally healed you really are. It was only after breaking up with Alessandro that I felt like a truly free and liberated woman. My relationship with him gave me wings, gave me courage and the strength to be independent."

"Yes, I remember how you bloomed every day" she says. "There was a radian glow all about you."

"When life brought Fulvio into my path" I continued, "I thought 'I am God, I have worked through all issues, nothing can catch me off-guard.' And see, I was God, until he didn't call me all day. Then my divinity evaporated. Then I thought: "This man is showing me how much work I still have ahead of me.' I remember it vividly. My first question when I saw Fulvio and fell in love with him at first sight was: 'What does this guy have to teach me?' Without other people, we can't ever truly know and love each other."

"What is this book about?"

"It's about the transformative power of relationships. Every relationship that comes our way has great potential to transform us. If we only approach the other person consciously, responsibly and with love, we have a chance to get to know and love ourselves. The book is also about different faces of love that bring growth and heal. How you can become stronger when you start with the most important thing: self-love. Until you reach that state or step on that path, all your relationships can be toxic, exhausting and heartbreaking."

Gratitude

I'm so grateful! Such wonderful things are happening!

I met Monika, we set up a company, got everything going and suddenly I started writing. I used to love writing, but I got discouraged because all my school essays were too long. Teachers would tell me: "Iwona, edit it, it's too long, it's not a book, it's an essay. You have to tighten it somehow." So I tightened things up to adapt to generally applicable rules and norms. Then I wrote diaries, but unfortunately one day I caught my mother reading them, so I stopped writing.

How did I come back to writing?

One of many lonely evenings without contact with Fulvio, when I missed him very much wonderful thoughts came to me. Feelings of love and nostalgia combined with the happiness of adoration and gratitude for having him. I felt sad that I couldn't hug him, that I couldn't feel what I always feel when he holds me in his arms. I scrolled through our WhatsApp conversations, listened to all our recordings and looked at photos. I was reenergized by the moments of happiness I received from him. I remembered Julia's words: "Don't wait, act."

An idea came to my mind: My love, I will write you a poem.

I will write poems to you and post them on FB. You won't even know that they belong to you. This will be my sweet secret.

I fired up the computer, started Word and wrote the first lines: "One look...". Before I knew it, the poem turned into prose. I wrote automatically, from the heart, I wrote about how I felt.

Writing gave me peace and solace.

After a few days, the thought of the book came to my mind and I felt an irresistible need to share this text. "Who should I write to?" I ponder, and Gosia immediately comes to mind. I sent her one of the working chapters and waited.

After a few minutes, feedback comes from far-away London:

"Iwonka! Oh, my God! Thank you so much for sharing this with me. You know, my dear, you have such incredible way with words. You show such a normal, average life in such a wonderful way. When I listen to you, I have the impression that life is beautiful. Thank you! I feel honored. I love you."

The next day I call Mark, who was my boyfriend when we were both in our twenties, but who is now my friend. I ask:

"Dear would you have a moment for me? I would like to read something to you."

"No problem, darling" he says. "I'm in the car right now, on my way home from work. I have time to listen."

I immerse myself in reading, and when I finish, there is silence on the other end of the phone.

"Hello are you there?" – I ask abashed.

"Yes I'm here" he responds. "Iwonka, that's wonderful. When you started reading, I was sure that you had bought an interesting book and I even wanted to ask about its title. After a while, when the facts from the book began to intertwine with events from your life, I thought: 'Unbelievable! She stumbled upon a book about her life.' The longer you read, the more I thought 'Oh dang, that's a work of art!' Keep writing, my dear, but do leave me more recordings of what you wrote, because it's wonderful to listen to."

After hearing what I heard, tears well up in my eyes and I feel that I have truly found my place.

I have so much gratitude for everything that's happening around me.With small, sometimes painful steps I am moving in a new direction, one I hadn't even seen in my most beautiful dreams. I never suspected that I would write books and that someone would want to read them.

I am grateful for this gift of putting my thoughts and emotions on paper.

I'm grateful that this is happening, even though I didn't plan it.

My life is unfolding like a complex jigsaw puzzle, its pieces seemingly strewn in haphazard chaos, each one refusing to slot into place. As I sit on the carpet, my gaze lost in the kaleidoscope of fragments before me, all I see is a disjointed mess. But when I rise and look down, the pieces began to merge into a coherent picture, revealing a pattern I hadn't seen before. It was nothing short of a miracle, a testament to the wondrous things that unfold when you thaw the ice around your heart and open yourself to the possibilities of love and emotion.

I am grateful to Ania Ewa Suska for organizing Mentoring for Women, in the first edition of which I took part. I was still in a relationship and trying to find my calling and the meaning of life. My dear Mentor – all those tears of despair, sadness and hopelessness shed while doing homework were the beginning of the melting of my glacier.

I am grateful to my ex for daring to leave me in March. My dear, thanks to your decision our toxic dance ended, because I would never have dared to do it. If it weren't for you, I wouldn't have received the gift of a second life.

I am grateful to Gosia Gorna, whose therapy dissuaded me from making the worst life decision I have ever thought about. Gosia, you are great. I am grateful for the months of working together, which showed me that the greatest treasure in life is love. Remember back in March when you told me I would write a book? I didn't believe it. You also told me that my books would be read by women and would give them hope for love and joy in life, that I would meet women and inspire them to change their thinking and actions. And it has already happened, my love. It's already happened. I owe my life to Gosia, I will write about that in my next book.

I am extremely grateful to Alessandro, my first Italian beau who woke up my femininity, who made me feel like a million dollars for the first time in my life and helped me to blossom day by day. Thank you my dear friend. While being with you I fell in love with myself.

Many wonderful things have happened since my transformation began. For example, my friend Dorotka Kasprzyk from the Mentoring Women group asks me:

“Girl, what are you doing? I haven't seen you for a month, how are there so many new things happening for you. How did you make that happen?”

And I calmly answer:

“The greatest thing, my dear, is that I didn’t make it happen. It all came to me and I just didn’t run away from it. I'm not spinning any plans. It’s fate that puts different people in my path, and changes follow the people. I just participate in it with confidence and watch as a beautiful solitaire game is built from the new deck of cards.”

I am grateful that the universe put the therapist Julia Szczepaniszyn on my path, thanks to whom I discovered more “skeletons” in the closet called life, and who gave me the courage to fall in love.

Dear, thank you for such a deep and spiritual therapy, filled with love and respect for other people.

I am grateful to everyone who came into my old and new life, whether they came only for a moment or stayed longer.

In particular, I’m grateful to all of the men who allow me to see who and where I am.

To Fulvio, the remarkable man whose entrance into my life this summer sparked the creation of these pages.

Baby! My gratitude for your presence in my life is boundless. You have not only allowed me to fall in love, but you have also become my muse. In the depths of your eyes, I see an ocean of love, enveloping me in its warm, comforting embrace, like a soft, fluffy cloud. Each day with you is a journey through intense emotions, thawing layers of my being, revealing depths I never knew existed. My love, you are an immeasurable gift, and this book is a testament to the inspiration you've ignited within me. Thank you, for everything.

I am grateful for how courageously you embrace the universe's design for my life, and the artful, graceful way you manage to get under my skin. My hat is off to you, Fulvio, for your unwavering commitment and daily dedication to nurturing my talents into full bloom. It's a shame you don't recognize the gifted therapist you naturally are.

My dear, you are undeniably the progenitor of this book. This creation is not just mine; it's our joint endeavor, our shared offspring. Filled with love – my sweet.

I am extremely grateful to the universe for the opportunity to feel powerful love.

My Dear, I am grateful to you for deciding to follow the flow that lured you, even though you did not know the destination.

The lesson I learned is: Gratitude is the key to happiness

The lesson you learned is:

Notes From My Readers

My Reader – a being like me.

Iwona, I must tell you that you are an inspiration to me, my dear. Because I also went through a time, after breaking up with my partner, when my demons caught up with me and said: "You're fifty-two years old, who will want you with those wrinkles on your face? Who will love you? Who will want a woman who is going through menopause? Who will desire you? All the guys are younger than you, they have wives, children. You will end up with some fat and bald asshole. It's better to be alone."

When I look at you, I regain hope for elation, for falling in love and for feeling like a woman again. Watching your transformation is a huge gift. I never suspected that I would witness your such a spectacular transformation into a beautiful Angel.

G.

Iwona, talking to you is more than just a nice time. It's a conversation of the heart that brings clarity to things that are difficult to understand. You are amazing. You are a great gift.

Monika

Your book goes beyond telling a simple story. It's like talking to a friend. It's like listening to a woman who is like me - sometimes strong, but also delicate and sensitive to even the slightest gust of the winds of life. This book triggered many processes in me. It has moved me to examine my attitude towards people, especially men. I saw them as beings who are lost and in need of love, just like we are. How beautifully you describe your closeness to Fulvio, how honestly you share your experiences and with what love you talk about difficulties - it's a revelation.

I have always said that the most beautiful stories are written by life itself.

Alexandra

Can the flutter of a butterfly's wings change the world?

This book is like the touch of a butterfly. It brings a smile, awakens tenderness and releases previously unexpressed happiness. It also awakens the desire for something more.

I deeply believe that the world can only be changed in one way - by starting with ourselves. So if you feel that it's time to awaken your sensitivity, gain an appetite for life and stand in the fullness of your feminine power, I recommend Iwona's story about her life and transformation from a larva cocooned in her own limitations to a beautiful butterfly that delights and inspires others.

A.

Iwona's book reminded me that there is a great world of sensations, senses and female energy to which I closed myself off, but which is still waiting for me and without which my life is not complete. The chapters were like the touch of a butterfly on a July day, bringing happiness and the impression that life can be magical. It awakened the gentleness in me and freed me until now unexpressed desires hiding in the deepest recesses of the soul. Thanks to Iwona's stories about her life, I gained an appetite for life and began to become fully empowered as a woman.

Aldona Oklińska
Life coach

I am very grateful that you trusted me and shared your book with me before it saw the light of day. I was very moved while reading it. I felt these emotions in my body. For me it was a mixture of longing, admiration and a slight hint of jealousy. I admire you and at the same time I am a bit jealous that you gave yourself the space and freedom to experience and describe your emotions, feelings and passions. I admire you for your readiness and courage to fall in love with a man, with all the risks it entails. I still lack the courage to build a relationship with a man. I am already quite a self-aware woman. I got to know many of my fears and deficits and I have been working on them for a long time. However, I still fear rejection. I know that this is a huge block for me, but I haven't found a way to free myself from it yet... I admire your readiness to build a relationship with a man, to experience what is beautiful and difficult in being with another person.

I have great admiration for you for your readiness to stand in the truth.

Julita

Brave and attentive. By showing herself - without veils, make-up or masks - she shows us how to embrace the world with our whole self. How, if we consciously tap into our feelings, we can sail joyfully through the monotonous ocean of everyday life, thanks to extraordinary moments we encounter.

Entertaining and light, this work seeps into us and heals us, providing a mirror in which we can see ourselves. The question is, how much courage do we have to look at ourselves in love?

Absorbing, fascinating and disturbingly honest.

Monika

Dear Iwona, you touched me so much with your story! Your life tranformed from a an ordinary life story, to a tragedy, so that it could end up being a most wonderful love story. Never give up! It's such a banal and simple message, but how difficult it is to do it in life's difficult moments! You rose like a phoenix from the ashes, flew on wings of an Angel toward your happiness. Way to go! Thank you also for your trust in letting me be one of the first readers of this work - your love stories, life transformations, events that inspire. It made a huge impression on me. Your pen is light, but gets to heart of the matter. It touches the heart, emotions and moves you to tears. It's not just your story anymore. This is your mission! And now sail on the seas and oceans of human hearts and praise the name of the Polish woman!

Marek Klepacki

Dear Iwona, thank you for publishing this book even though it was tough in moments. I am extremely grateful to you for talking so honestly and openly about our fall in love with Fulvio and what it brought with it. I am very proud of you and I hope that thanks to you, thousands of women will believe that life is not always easy, but it is beautiful. Let's do everything to make your relationship with a man, instead of a societal expectation, a wonderful addition to an interesting and inspiring life.

Remember. Everything that is valuable is within you. You're a kick-ass woman!

It's a great honor for me to be you.

Iwona Kulwicka

How Does It All Work?

INFATUATION

We are here to fully experience our highest potential and learn all the lessons that will bring us closer to our true nature - to become love.

Everything that is not love will be shown to us and we will be given the choice of what to do with it. We will be put in various situations in which we will learn: how to love, what is toxic and what is mature, healthy and balanced love.

* * *

Our souls are drawn to each other to experience different lessons and learn love in different guises. We often meet people from other incarnations to complete certain karmic obligations and then we have the impression that we have known someone for centuries (as this may be the case). No matter how a relationship turns out, it is always good to start and end it with respect and love to dissolve our karmic obligations.

Sometimes we experience love that is full of passion, ups and downs, which is like a drug that is addictive and pumps hormones into our system that look like great love. This crazy love cannot also be an addiction and a reflection of the wounds that exist and are waiting for healing.

These are often the wounds of a rejected child who feels inadequate and would do anything to finally feel unconditional love and solace.

Throughout our lives we will experience love in various forms. Love for parents, for children, falling madly in love, mature love for a partner. What we desire most in life is to love and be loved. This feeling gives meaning to our existence and gives us a sense of happiness and joy.

The most important kind of love is the one that changes everything. It's love for our self.

Without it, we can spend our whole lives forever looking for someone who will fill our inner void. Someone who will finally take away from us this feeling of an undefined lack, this feeling of hunger, longing for what we have never given ourselves - unconditional love, respect and care.

When we burden our partner with the obligation to fill the gap of love, the acceptance we crave, and meet all our needs - even the ones we're not aware of - such a relationship is doomed. It is our responsibility to take care of ourselves, our needs and desires. When we learn to take care of our inner child and take full responsibility for feeling good, then we have a greater chance of having a relationship that is more mature, happy and long-lasting. A relationship which builds us up, nourishes us and in which there is the right amount of space to be together and to be apart, depending on the needs of each partner.

We get to a place of full acceptance, respect and love for each other by experiencing relationships with other people. Thanks to them, we get to know ourselves and find out who we really are. We experience our shadow, our dark side, which is waiting patiently for our attention and love.

In relationships, we discover what we want, what is good for us, and what burns us out. How we want to be touched, what resonates with us and gives us joy. We learn what strengthens us and what saps our power. We learn what happens when we love someone so much that we lose ourselves and stop noticing our own needs. A love relationship is an amazing dance that can bring wonderful lessons to our lives. However, the most important thing is that we take responsibility for our part, which we create consciously and unconsciously. Each of us is here to do our homework. We are here to learn who we are – to move further up the ladder of our self-development.

Moments of falling in love are turning points when everything can change - depending on what contract we have with the soul of a given person and what lessons we have to learn.

In these moments, the universe invites us to dance, which can be beautiful if we allow ourselves to be present in our body and heart, to take care of ourselves and the other person. Dancing requires letting go and mindfulness. Following your heart and listening to your body and that of the other person.

When entering a new relationship, it is worth remembering that...

DRUG

At the beginning, falling in love is like a drug and we may not think rationally and logically for some time.

When we fall in love, we can experience chemical changes that have a huge impact on our brain. When a relationship doesn't go our way or our partner leaves us, it seems like the absolute end of the world.

The better you understand what is happening chemically in your body, the faster you will be able to overcome a situation in which a state of despair may seem unsurvivable. When you fall in love, substances are produced that lead to a temporary brain fog. In its structure and action, falling in love is similar to amphetamine - it has intoxicating properties, causing a feeling of euphoria, joy, excitement and self-confidence of the person in love. On the other hand, it causes insomnia, anxiety, appetite disorders, lack of breath and concentration, and increased heart rate. Adrenaline regulates the secretion of other neurotransmitters related to emotions in the brain: noradrenaline, dopamine and serotonin, and also affects the release of β-endorphin, an opioid peptide responsible for feeling pleasure and providing bliss.

Norepinephrine (NA)

Norepinephrine is produced in the brain and nerve cells of the spinal cord, but the main place of its production is the adrenal medulla. It increases the pressure and force of myocardial contraction and dilates the pupils. Noradrenaline causes excitement, euphoria and a surge of good energy. It speeds up the heartbeat, raises blood pressure and causes you to blush at the sight of a loved one.

Dopamine

Dopamine and the reward system play an important role in creating bonds between partners. This neurotransmitter is very important in creating feelings of belonging and love between two people. The release of dopamine is stimulated by touch and increases during sex and orgasm. Too much dopamine may cause emotional dependence on others, which may ultimately lead to the formation of toxic relationships.

It is believed that the effect of dopamine is so pleasant that its drop during a painful breakup is like a drug withdrawal syndrome for our brain.

Serotonin (5-hydroxytryptamine, 5-HT)

As dopamine levels increase, the amount of serotonin in the brain decreases rapidly. It is normally responsible for healthy sleep and a sense of peace, impulsive behavior and sexual needs. Its deficiencies cause general distraction and lack of concentration. A person in love becomes confused and falls into extreme moods, depression and aggressive behavior may occur.

BE CAREFUL NOT PUT YOUR PARTNER ON A PEDESTAL

Anyone you place too high may fall from that place one day. It is worth having a balanced view of any given person - attributes and demerits. When you have a balanced perception of a person, you are more likely to have a long-term relationship.

If you perceive only positives, it is not a real image of the person.

Ask yourself how you feel, what you need at the moment - from yourself and from another person. Learn to communicate your needs and ask what the other person needs. Make sure to take care of yourself and do what you feel in your heart is right for you. Don't expect the other person to make you feel safe or will be your only source of happiness and joy.

When you start criticizing your partner often, see what attributes of yours are reflected in the mirror. Consider if it may be time to work on in yourself…

Tell the other person what you are grateful for and also what you need.

Love yourself more and take care of your joy. If you are happy, you will more easily attract someone with whom you will be even happier.

Gosia Gorna
Information Coach,
Author of the book "The Expansion Game"

From a Man's Point of View

"The protection of an awakened woman in the presence of a man is the greatest mirror of where he truly is in his spiritual journey.

This does not mean that a man is dependent on a woman to achieve a high level of consciousness, but it does mean that the divine feminine is the greatest and strictest mirror of where he truly is in his journey."

Bartek Stefański, "Medicine of Life"

Whether you want to sleep with a woman, marry a woman, or have a deep relationship, it will fail if she doesn't feel safe. Security is the most important quality you can offer a woman because it allows her to feel fully with you and freely explore her divine, feminine nature.

In all relationships, the masculine dynamic is the energy leader. I use the word masculine because this dynamic does not exclude any sexual orientation. When two women or men are together, one person will inhabit the masculine magnetic pole more and the other will act as the feminine pole, because we all have masculine and feminine energy within us. In most heterosexual relationships, the man inhabits the male magnetic pole. As the male partner, it is your responsibility to create a safe ground in which your partner can blossom and feel nurtured to reveal her full self - from dark and destructive goddess to goddess of light.

This means that you have room for all of her expressions, even those that your mind labels as less beautiful or alluring. If you refuse to create a safe ground for your partner, your love life will fail because she will not feel emotionally and spiritually connected to you. Only when you truly inhabit your authentic core – whether masculine or feminine – will you be able to create a blissful relationship. This is not a role you have to fill. It is your authentic nature, your deepest gift of life and love.

Women have been suppressed for years. They went through collective trauma because they were not treated equal to men. Women were called witches, whores, bitches and many other unsavory names that have left a deep mark on our consciousness. Nearly 400 years ago in Europe, about 50,000 people were burned at the stake, 80% of them were women. Almost all religions suppress the feminine, even those commonly considered "sacred" or innocent. Although much has fortunately changed in today's world, there is still a struggle for pay equity in the corporate world, for bodily autonomy, and also on a spiritual level, as femininity is still suppressed by the shadow of societies ruled mainly by men.

If you, as a partner, don't have empathy or understand where she comes from and what she has been through, you will experience a lot of discord and she will not feel safe. It's not easy for a woman to trust you and it's not easy for her to open up fully to you Acknowledge this, lead her to her beautiful heart, encourage her to open up, make sure she is safe and fully protected, and then she will begin to blossom. Then and only then will she be able to surrender to her feminine magnetic pole.

Most men don't know that when a woman feels truly safe, she will feel endless inspiration. Femininity filled me with purpose, passion and a deep desire to serve the world with my authentic gifts as a man. Making her feel safe is a journey that will bring out the best in both of you.

So how do you make a woman feel safe? First, you must be fully present. "Be present" or "be here and now" have become important slogans in personal development and spiritual community. Being present does not mean that you are enlightened or experiencing altered states of consciousness. It simply means that you are not stuck in your head, but that you are in your body. Not getting stuck in your head means being aware of your surroundings, your breath, the scents you smell, the many signs the universe offers you through ordinary everyday interactions.

When men don't practice being present, they lose themselves in the pornography, in nightclubs or computer games. In fact, they long to feel alive, to feel their truth, to penetrate the world with their presence. Women feel safe with men who are fully present. The moment you get stuck in your head, she will detect it and then she won't be able to fully open up to you.

The fastest way to become present is to connect with your breath. You cannot stay in your head when you are aware of your breathing. Breathe deeply, fill your entire belly as you inhale, and breathe through your spine as you exhale.

Each time you realize that she doesn't feel safe or seems irritated, connect with your breathing instead of trying to find a solution in your head. Your words and actions are important, but your state of presence has a profound impact on a woman.

The awakened warrior's greatest weapon is presence, and each day he sharpens it with his breath, listening deeply to both his soul and the universe. When life gets challenging, he knows his only refuge and shield is his fierce presence. The moment he becomes fully present, his sword cuts through all doubts, all fears, leaving him with only his authentic truth.

You can practice being present at any moment in your life, with a partner or on your own. The more you practice being in the moment when you arc alone, the easier it will be to be present with her. Of course, financial and physical security are elements that she also values. However, your presence is at the top of the pyramid of needs. Without it, your intimate relationship cannot be nurtured and it withers like a flower in the dark.

Bartek Stefański

An Interview with My Sister

Iwona: I would like to interview you about my big transformation, which has no end in sight. I would like to go back to March this year and ask you - do you remember the day I called you and told you that my ex had left me?
Aleksandra: Yes, I remember that day clearly. I was very happy then. First of all, I'm glad you contacted me. I was waiting for a call from you because I already knew about your situation from our aunt. She asked me if I had contact with you and said she was worried because he left you. I felt sorry for you then. But secondly, I was happy because I always thought that you weren't yourself around him. That you were lost with him. And then I thought that if I could, I would like to help you and have you come to me. So when you called me, I thought that I could fulfill my plan to bring you to my place and have you with me.

We hadn't seen each other for a long time, several years...
Yes, we'd lost contact with each other almost completely. Well... in my opinion he didn't suit you at all. I thought that you were on the losing end of this relationship... And I thought this was "the moment". This was the moment when you should finally become independent from him.

And tell me, what was I like during these twenty-four years?
I will use the words of my son, Kostek, because they illustrate it well. He once said: "Mom, are like a miniature pinscher, and Aunt Iwona is a pit-

bull." Kostek always thought that you were a person with great charisma; that you knew what you wanted; but also that you were quite uncompromising, sharp. Do you remember when I had a big problem and my children couldn't cope with me? They called you because you were their last resort to snap me out of it. For me, you were a person who was, on the one hand, very down to earth, but on the other hand, you were also a bit uncompromising. I had the impression that you were very much like your boyfriend and you took on a part of him, maybe not so much his personality, but his views. You were losing yourself in all this, you know?

I know. And you're right.
You compared yourself to others a lot, and you could even be a little ruthless. We could rely on you because you could handle anything, you had inexhaustible energy and were so resourceful. But it was all devoid of… Emotion? I remember when you came to see me when Kostek called you. On the one hand, you had a lot of understanding and empathy for me, but on the other, you were so... Principled. You know what I mean?

Yes, I was like a robot. Cold, frozen.
Yes, you were frozen. But I could always count on you, I always knew I could rely on you. However, you were also easily influenced by a man. As if you didn't believe in yourself, as if you were only defined by what your man represented.

Do you remember what you said when you invited me to Modena?
I remember. It was only a few words, because I didn't even want to talk too much. I told you: "Pack your stuff, come, I will show you what real life can be like."

Is that why you invited me?
I felt your sadness, your despair, but I also felt that I could pull you out of it. So that you could experience, at least for a moment, a nice little life.

I wanted to show you something other than the one you had known for the previous twenty-four years.

I was also in a significant period of my life, because I had moved from Poland to Italy. I really needed this change, but it wasn't until I got here that I realized how much I needed it. Such a complete change. It took me out of one life and threw me into another one where I didn't know anyone, not even the language. When you called me, I had already lived here for six months, and I started to feel more at home with everything: this newness, Italy, the fact that a beautiful spring was beginning here. I felt a lot of energy and great strength coming from the change I had made. And I really wanted to show it to you.

I thought that this would allow you to completely change your perspective and see that there is a different life. I felt you could benefit from staying here. You can calm your mind and think things through. That I would give you space so you wouldn't have to worry.

I also know that you don't like being alone, that you need people. And even though I felt good being on my own and single, I also felt loneliness and the need to be with someone close to me. Even though we no longer had the same contact as before, you were very dear to me, so I thought this could be good for you, but also good for me, and that we would be able to get closer to each other again thanks to your stay here.

That was a great idea, sister. Both mine for having the courage and calling you, and yours for inviting me. Yes, I also remember my fear that our separation was too long for us to get closer to each other again. But fortunately it remained only a fear. What changes have you noticed in me since March until now?

They're astronomical! I think you have outgrown the "master", assuming that by inviting you and saying: "You will get to know a different life", I felt like I was introducing you to it, I felt like I was your master in this topic. When you came here, I wanted you to see that you can have a different relationship with guys. That you can have fun with guys, that you can have pleasure in relationships with them, that you can flirt.

And then I told you about Tinder. I remember how clumsy you were at the beginning, and I will never forget how you approached it. Like an exam! You worried that people would judge you on there. And your question, can you send someone a kiss on Tinder if you don't know them? Won't that make him think you're easy? This is how you started, and now I see how much you have opened up to experiences, to your femininity.

I noticed that part of your change is that you have become physically very feminine. You grown your hair long, you are very beautiful. You are maturing into your femininity. In the past I didn't feel this energy inside you. Now I feel that you are not only very feminine, but also wise.

Before I knew intellectually that you were a wise woman, but now that wisdom emanates from you in every conversation. The cold that used to be there and that made you so withdrawn is absolutely gone. You are very open, understanding, empathetic and feminine. I think I even told you recently that I'm getting to know you again. It's like I'm meeting a new person I've known my whole life.

Yes, I feel it too, my love, and every day I am more and more amazed by how much you can change thanks to love. First by the one you receive, and then by the one you learn to give. Love followed by empathy and respect. And do you remember what you told me in Modena? That you got someone back.

Of course. As a child, you were an older sister to me, and then life happened and you sort of took on the role of my mother. When you visited me in March, it felt more like my relationship with my mother. And then I told you that I got my sister back. We were no longer in a relationship in which I felt deference, in which I had to have respect, because it was a relationship with a "mom", but we were on the same level. Yes, I felt like I had a sister again. Relationships between sisters are completely different. The relationship with your mother is, above all, about a sense of security. I felt that with you for many years. Now I have a feeling of understanding and closeness to a person who not only wishes me well, but also understands me as if they were me. It's an even deeper connection.

The change in our relationship was also a huge surprise and pleasure for me. A surprise, because I didn't suspect that I would ever be able to give advice to people from a peer perspective, and not as a teacher. Pleasure, because I definitely prefer this type of relationship. It is devoid of any kind of self-aggrandizement or dictating what someone should, or shouldn't do. I am glad that in conversations with people I no longer feel the need to say: "you must", "you should", "you have to". I finally regained my lightness. Alex, so who am I to you now? After the transformation I've gone through so far?
You are my best friend, you are my sister. You are not only my sister, but also the best sister I could ever dream of. You are simply the closest person to me. I don't have such closeness with anyone else, such openness, such trust. Sometimes I talk to you like a mirror in which I can look at myself because I trust you completely. When we talk, I know that you are talking to me objectively and that you don't want to compromise anything. I really feel your focus on me. So you are the closest person to me. And that has just changed. I mean, you were already close to me because you were my family, but I want to be with someone out of my own need, not out of a sense of obligation. And now you are the closest person to me because I want it and I feel that you are the closest to me, not because you are my cousin, or because you are family.

And to what extent do you think my falling in love influenced this change?
I think it was a process. I believe that your change was definitely influenced by your breakup with your ex and the fact that you did something about it. You started to focus on yourself, you started reaching out for advice and guidance.

You mean I went into therapy?

You entered therapy, but not the traditional kind, rather the one related to energy and self-understanding. Then it all evolved. I think that meeting Fulvio accelerated your transformation, but... I think that your change was primarily influenced by the fact that you started writing this book. And the reason that triggered you to start doing this was Fulvio. So it's all connected. I wouldn't separate it, because if you were only in love with Fulvio, you would probably be looking for a way out of this love in therapy and how to deal with it. However, it seems to me that you no longer wanted to look for therapy outside, but inside yourself... The result of which is this book. It helps you understand yourself even better, to convey something from within. This is like another piece in your change puzzle. So I can't say what impact your falling in love with Fulvio had, because I think it's already the result of the change you've been going through since March. That you allowed yourself to fall in love thanks to this. And since there was just the man you could fall in love with, you could move on. Go into your own development, into your change. I also wouldn't consider Fulvio as the key moment of your change. He is part of the whole process and you needed him at this moment. To make you open up, completely unfreeze, allow yourself to fall in love. I also think that if this relationship had turned out differently, you would probably have written this book anyway, but you would have needed it for something different than now. Besides, I think that you are not the only one who really needs this book. I feel that you wrote it with the intention of giving others what you have gained since March. That you wanted to share it all. Therefore, in my opinion, there are two spaces in which this book works.

Yes. This is my therapy, but I also hope to help others.

Yes. This is you sharing the wisdom, ideas and insights you received during this short but very intense time. How many women find themselves in such a situation? Women who love too intensly; women who cannot cope with their feelings; women for whom there is only an “all or nothing" approach to relationships. There are plenty of them and I believe that this book is not only your therapy, but also an aid for other women.

I really hope that this is how the book will be received. My love, you are the person who walked hand in hand with me on this one. You actually started all this with me and you will continue with me. Because it's not over yet. We don't really know when that will be, and we'll probably talk about that in my next book as well.
I hope so because I think you should pass on your wisdom widely. This is how I perceive your book. That there is simply wisdom in this story, from which everyone can take as much as they want. Dearest, you are my motivation and inspiration. When I have weaker moments, I just look at your change and think to myself: "God, if Iwona was able to do so much in six months, if I even accomplish ten percent of it, I will be the champion of the world." For example, for me, writing one sentence that makes sense and expresses something, and another person reading it is able to understand it, is truly a great struggle. And you wrote thousands of these sentences. I see how passionate you are about it and how it hooked you. And this is also a huge motivation for me, a light in a dark tunnel. Since half a year ago no one even thought about the fact that you could write, and here you are just finishing a book! So I also think to myself: "Damn, maybe there is still something like this in front of me, I just haven't found it yet. But I can do it, just like you did."

Oh yes. I truly believed that there were things we simply never dreamed of.
One more thing. My dear, I have known you since birth; I knew you later in my adult life; then I reconnected with you now, during the transformation; but I will tell you that in this book I discovered another you. I'm getting to know you even more. I am very happy about where you are and look to your future with calm. Your transformation is a change from a woman who was extremely dependent on another person to a truly independent one. Like everyone else, you still have your "bad days" and

“those moments”, but you have changed a lot. You started to be your real self. The person you really are inside.

Yes, although this change is ongoing. We need time to change.
That's true. At the same time, I don't think we ever change enough to be able to say, “job done.” It's just important to go in the right direction. In a direction that’s healthy for us. The most important thing is to reach a stage where we feel good about ourselves.

What’s Next?

It is the woman who chooses a man to process her problems and traumas with him.

Monday. The sixth day of my COVID self isolation. I miss Fulvio. We haven’t spoken since Saturday.

That Friday I send him a text message:

“Dearest! I know you're busy and I don't expect an immediate response. I do not feel well. I still have a very high fever and strange cough. I called the doctor and he told me that I should treat Covid like a common cold, and if I start having breathing problems, I should call an ambulance. But that's not the hardest thing for me, because I know that the disease will pass. I don't know why, but while sick with Covid I feel mentally weaker than ever before. I feel very lonely and I need your support. Maybe it's the result of our recent misunderstanding? Maybe it's something else? I don't know. The last situation also upset me. I realized that a stupid misunderstanding could have separated us and I could have lost the man I love so much and to whom I am so close.

I'm very confused. Maybe I'm not thinking straight?

I remembered that before I left for Bologna, we had such a deep connection that we would pick up WhatsApp and write to each other at the exact same time. Just two weeks ago I knew when he was thinking about me and when he was about to text me. I would get a feeling seconds before I received the message. However, a week ago I lost it. It doesn't seem like a big deal, just a signal out of nowhere that something has changed.

I add to my message:

"I'd like you to tell me if still wait for my "Good morning" every morning. What really happened? Please be honest. Tell me. Do you need more time to get back into a happy place or is it something else? I feel that your behaviour has changed and that it happened even before this misunderstanding with the photo. I felt it a few days beforehand. Maybe it's just my imagination, or maybe it's my intuition, please let me know. Have a lovely day."

This message, like many others, remained unanswered.

In order not to lose my mind, I returned to an old technique, unfortunately recently forgotten by me, which helps me to redirect my thinking and allows me to face what I am afraid of.

Listen:

Even though I don't want to lose Fulvio, I love and respect myself. Even though I want to be with him so much, I let him go because he has already pushed me so much. He did what he was supposed to do and even more than I expected. I am allowing this relationship to shut down and end.

And I look forward to it with joy. [Deep inhale, then exhale.]

I also allow myself to let this relationship begin now, for us to start communicating very sincerely and deeply, and for him to see who I really am and reveal himself to me as well. So that he can find more time for me, for himself and for his life.

And I look forward to it with joy. [Deep inhale, then exhale.]

I allow Fulvio to actually be offended by me and for him to fall out of love with me and to fall from my pedestal, and for him to show me the other side of him, someone who is limited in trustworthiness, who has no time for himself and for others, for me .

And I look forward to it with joy. [Deep inhale, then exhale.]

But I also give myself permission for this to turn into something wonderful and for us to find a new way of communicating. For him to trust me and for our relationship to transform. So that we can start fully being ourselves and start enjoying ourselves. So that we can go beyond pushing and celebrate being together in person.

And I look forward to it with joy. [Deep inhale, then exhale.]

But I also accept it if this is the end. I accept that Fulvio led me to the door he was supposed to lead me to, and my soul initiated all of this to free him and free myself. I open myself to another, even more amazing door that will open and for miracles to happen that I didn't expect - with Fulvio or with someone else.

I allow myself incredible joy and happiness. [Deep inhale, then exhale.]

I also allow the situation with Fulvio to teach me another lesson and I allow him to do what is best for him.

And I look forward to it with great joy.

* * *

After a few go-rounds, you feel that nothing can surprise you in life anymore. You slowly regain inner peace and trust that everything will turn out as it should.

Today, for the first time, I felt such incredible peace. Of course I miss Fulvio. When I recall his image, I hold it close to my heart and feel grateful for everything he has given me. I also have a lot of understanding for his behavior and... compassion. Although no, "compassion" is not the right word. Maybe "understanding" is the key word. I also have understanding for his difficulties in communicating with me.

And I am overwhelmed with such mercy and I feel so sorry that he cannot muster the courage to talk to me. I am full of love.

A CONVERSATION WITH THE SOUL

Dear Fulvio,

I loved you very much and I was in love with you. I'm thankful for it all. To me you are beautiful, attractive and I love being with you. I would love to continue this relationship and friendship because we haven't reached its full potential, but I respect any decision you make. I love you, I respect you, I see you, I hear you and I wish for you with a wonderful life, joy, happiness and contentment. May your life be beautiful. Celebrate it with me or someone else. I love you.

* * *

Seventh day of my quarantine, at 8:51 am I am woken up by a phone call.

"Who is calling?" You ask. Fulvio!

"Hi, sweety…"

* * *

A woman awake?

What bings me peace? The basis of peace is achieving such a balance that the relationship is only a wonderful addition to my life, and not its only meaning. When I reach this level, I will treat every breakup as the end of a certain wonderful stage of my life. No panic, no regrets and no judgments. Then I will think: "I am in love, I'm spending time with a wonderful man, I am with him and I am happy, but when the love ends, I will accept it serenly!"

Wiem, nie będę się już dłużej bać, już nie tańczę do melodii, którą znam. Jestem wolna, już mnie porwał wiatr. Daleko, gdzie mleko rozlewa się...

Moja wersja tekstu piosenki „I Ciebie też, bardzo"
Męskie Granie Orkiestra 2021

How to Partner With Me

I AM

I am and I feel the power flowing from this word.
I am in the here and now.
I am part of the Universe
I am a soul in a body and a body in a soul.
I am a combination of energy and matter. I am not here by accident
I am here for a reason. I am the wisdom of my experiences
I am the potential of my feelings and thoughts. I am the result of my choices
I am perfection in my imperfection. I am value in itself
I am already and I am still I am even when I have nothing
I am here even when no one pays attention to me. I am the light in the darkness
I am a breath in silence I am the creator of my life I am and I feel it in my heart
I am because you are, you are because I am

Claudia Pingot[1]

[1] Translated from original Polish. Find Claudia Pingot at klaudiapingot.pl

WHO AM I?

Privately - a happy woman and mother. I would even prefer the term: happy being.

No, I am not completely fulfilled, because that would mean that I no longer expect anything more from life than what I have already experienced. Meanwhile, I have an increasing appetite for life. I'm just planning my first trip to Africa and I'm already sure it won't be the last. What will I be doing there? Now I'm only going there as a tourist, but just this morning a new idea came to my mind - a new project "Africa".

HOW DID ALL OF THIS HAPPEN?

When I found out in March 2021 that my twenty-four-year relationship was over and I felt like I was at rock bottom. I asked for help.

It wasn't easy to admit that this intelligent, pretty and highly educated Iwonka - who always had everything under control - had problems. I had to face the truth and admit that although the walls I had built around me in order to survive years in a difficult relationship allowed me to function intellectualy, but deprived me of the ability to feel.

For an ambitious top student - who spent her whole life trying to prove that she could always do it - the greatest shame was admitting defeat, and the pain of losing was so great that life stopped having meaning for me.

Today, when I know that everything happens for a reason, I want to discover my talents, exceed the limits of my own possibilities and feel alive every day. To live for myself and for others. Live among people and for people.

AND PROFESSIONALLY?

Professionally - I'm the co-owner of IMONA, a business established to support women and their activities in business.

I discovered a long time ago that success comes from people. I am a supporter of running a business based on long-term relationships, respect, trust and contributing to local communities.

This company was born out of my great passion, which is working in administrative sciences. Thanks to my experience, I created my own SASED documentation recording system, the implementation of which guarantees entrepreneurs increased comfort in running their business.

IMONA means order in every business.

We deal with all aspects of company organization - from organizing documentation, through organizing office work and long-term customer support. Our solutions are designed to increase the efficiency of the administrative department and provide full oversight over company resources.

MY PLANS

My huge dream is to support women professionally also in their private lives. So far, I've done it for friends. My friends and colleagues like to ask me for advice and confide in me, saying that they feel like they are talking to their sister. In meetings with me, they value the sense of safety and having space to be themselves.

I am here to help women who, like me, have experienced difficult times and have lost faith in life and love.

I can guide you through seeing how relationships - even, or rather especially, those that we define as difficult - can be used in a wonderful way for your own transformation, so that you can

- love yourself,
- express what you feel and what you want,
- reject limiting beliefs,
- debunk myths,
- gain a sense of freedom,
- celebrate life through emotions, because they make us feel alive.

I will teach you how to dance with yourself, hold yourself tenderly like a mother holds her child, and say to yourself, "I love you. I am with you and I will always be with you."

I will show you how to accept your imperfections and support yourself in finding your path. How to look at yourself in the mirror every morning with love and respect for everything you have done and for what you didn't because you could not do otherwise.

I would like all my clients and readers to experience a complete transformation and fall in love with themselves, with life and with people. It will be my great pleasure to help them return to themselves and step into their power.

And I look forward to it with joy.

BIBLIOGRAPHY

1. Hugo, Victor. *Les Misérables (vol. 1)* from the Classic Novels series. Translated by Krystyna Byczewska. Warsaw: Prószyński and S-ka, 2004, p. 194.

2. Walkiewicz, Jacek. *Full Power of Possibilities*. Gliwice: Helion, 2015, pp. 10, 59.

3. Pingot, Klaudia. Facebook, https://www.facebook.com/SpecBabka/?locale=pl_.

4. Gorna, Gosia. *The Expansion Game: A powerful method to transform your fear into brilliance*, 2017.

5. Zawiałow, Daria; Podsiadło, Dawid; Bambino, Vito. *I ciebie też, bardzo.* Męskie Granie Orkiestra, 2021.

www.ingramcontent.com/pod-product-compliance
Lightning Source LLC
La Vergne TN
LVHW012034160826
845678LV00013B/2599

9788397063044